POPEYE LUCAS
Queenstown

⁓✻⁓

POPEYE LUCAS

Queenstown

by F. J. Lucas

A. H. & A. W. REED

Wellington   Auckland   Sydney

First published 1968

A. H. & A. W. REED
182 Wakefield Street, Wellington
29 Dacre Street, Auckland
51 Whiting Street, Artarmon, Sydney

Set in 11 on 13 point Baskerville "Monotype"
and printed and bound by
Cox & Wyman Ltd., London, Fakenham and Reading

dedicated to
My Wife

Contents

List of Illustrations

LIST OF ILLUSTRATIONS

Acknowledgments

I HAVE MANY PEOPLE to thank for help and encouragement with this book.

The files of the *Otago Daily Times*, the Dunedin *Evening Star*, the Wellington *Evening Post*, the *Southland Times*, and *Southland News*, the Christchurch *Star-Sun*, the *New Zealand Herald*, the *Central Otago News*, the *Weekly News*, *Better Business*, *Walkabout*, and *People* have been most useful.

Among the most valuable reference books have been *Reminiscences of a New Chum* by Charles F. Lucas, *Greenfield Pioneers* by L. E. Smith, and *Pioneers of Martins Bay* by Mrs Florence Mackenzie.

To those people who have allowed the use of their photographs (they are individually acknowledged in the List of Illustrations) I am also most grateful; and to Norman Forrest, who has helped with the final tidying-up of the text.

Thank you, all of you.

POPEYE

Cecil Peak, Queenstown

Introduction

LAST YEAR some 14,000 tourists, mostly Americans and Australians, but many New Zealanders too, visited us at Cecil Peak Station on the shores of Lake Wakatipu. Most tourists are keen to see a high-country farm, and most of them ask endless questions:

"Say, is this a sheep ranch?"

"Yes."

"Say, where are all the sheep? Hidin' in the hills?"

"Well, there's about 4,000 sheep up that side of the hill, and 4,000 up this side."

"Gee, I can't see them."

"Neither can I, but they're there all right."

"Yeah, well I saw some of 'em down at your factory at the dock, where we landed."

"That was our shearing shed at the jetty, sure."

"Yeah, and they sure looked funny with all their fur off."

"Eh? *Fur?* Oh yes, yes. . . !"

But even if some tourists don't know what's on a sheep's back (many of them do, of course) they are very welcome nevertheless. I don't mean just because of their almighty dollars; I do mean because my wife Lorie and I enjoy meeting them, talking to them – especially the few glum ones, whom we try to single out in our welcome, hoping to send them on their way in more cheerful mind. To be really friendly, you must be sincere, however, and I think that's as good an unofficial motto as we'll ever have.

When I come to think of it, I realise that catering for tourists, flying, and farming are the themes that have dominated my life.

I was born and grew up a farmer's son; but almost as soon as I reached adulthood I was off to join the Air Force. I spent 10 years of my life in the Services – and they were good years too – four in peacetime service and six in war.

After the war I heard the call of the land, but the message was premature, so it was back to the highways of the sky, this time in the hurly-burly of commercial aviation. Aerial farming came into it, however, and it was also spiced with a new interest – tourism by air.

Almost 14 years later the needs of my family, four boys and a girl, forced me to make a reappraisal. My way of life seemed to offer little for them so I decided to give up the flying game for something that I hoped would offer more stability for the future.

The decision was made not without regret; but looking back, I'm sure it was the right one. The family loved the new life from the very first, and now we are a fully occupied and united family, farming this bit of high country on the west side of Lake Wakatipu – and almost by accident we're back into tourism.

After seven years the boys are unmistakably farmer's sons, and our daughter is a farmer's wife. All this is as it should be – for it seems that farming is in our blood.

I

In the Blood

THERE'S NO DOUBT that farming *is* in the blood. My parents farmed 1,000 acres at Tuapeka Mouth, South Otago, called Moor Farm after my father's birthplace in England, and had another property just across the river at Tuapeka Mouth, which was called Cranleigh – named this time after Father's old school, Cranleigh College, in England.

He had emigrated to New Zealand as a boy of 16 and was one of a family of 12. His father had farmed a property of 500 acres, known as Moor Farm near Petworth, Sussex. Father and his 11 brothers and sisters were all born in the rambling, old, two-storied Elizabethan manor house.

The farm my father established in New Zealand had been part of the Greenfield estate, which the Government took over in 1904 to cut up for closer settlement. It was subdivided in 1905, and Father had been one of the lucky ballotees. My mother, Ethel Smith, was one of the daughters of James Smith of Greenfield, and grand-daughter of James Chapman Smith, founder of the estate; she married my father in 1909.

When Greenfield was taken over by the Government the property consisted of 33,000 acres, 24,000 of which my great-grandfather had freeholded. It was subdivided into 39 farms and one small grazing run, leaving my maternal grand-parents with about 2,000 acres, called the Homestead Block, upon which stood the original Greenfield homestead buildings.

Great-grandfather James Chapman Smith had retired to Dunedin in 1900, leaving his sons, my grandfather James and his brother John, to manage the property. Great-grandfather died in 1903, fortunately before he could see the estate cut up and the homestead shorn of all its land, and all his hard work and striving come to nothing within the next quarter of a century.

We children loved to visit Granny Smith as we called my maternal grandmother. In those days the Greenfield homestead still retained its dignity and charm. Handsome gates still showed the way to the long, sweeping drive lined by beautiful old trees, beneath which smart cobs and gigs still drove, as well as the early model cars, which were becoming increasingly popular, particularly with my mother's brothers. The winding pathways, landscaped banks and dells, the massed rhododendrons, camellias, and countless other shrubs and flowers were well tended, and the conservatory in good repair. There were still the Chinese gardeners, and the rambling, two-storied 28-roomed house, with its wide verandas screened by wistaria vines and banksia rose, still offered open-house hospitality to many people, distinguished and otherwise. The well-kept stables, the busy forge and smithy, the cookshop and dairy, all hummed with life and activity.

Changing conditions, falling prices and an economic depression made it impossible for my uncles to carry on, and eventually the property had to be sold up. That lovely old homestead was torn down and partly rebuilt elsewhere; the drive, shrubbery and gardens became no more; and where my grandmother had lovingly tended her plants, and successive Chinese had raked and hoed and planted, only a wilderness of self-sown trees remained. A stranger not knowing their past history, coming upon those impressive gates buried in a thicket of trees, marking the entrance to nowhere, might well wonder where he had got to.

Granny was the sort you read about in books, always smiling, kindly, and hospitable, waiting with a warm welcome on the wide front steps.

The house was full of pictures and books, many of them very valuable, and part of Great-grandfather's collection of original paintings and first editions. When we were children church services were held in the drawing-room, which was kept as a permanent chapel for the district. The Rev. Mr Richards, at that time vicar, would drive over from Lawrence to take the service. He was a kindly soul, and could never bring himself to use the whip on his horse, and so he was always late. On his arrival at Greenfield the Irish groom would take his horse gently enough round to the stables, but as soon as he was out of sight of the soft-hearted vicar, he'd whip it up into a smart trot, and after he had given it some vigorous exercise would reward it with a generous feed.

The vicar always drove back to Lawrence at a spanking trot, and frequently complimented Grandfather on the excellent oats he grew, convinced that these were responsible for the improved performance of his horse.

We teased the Chinese gardeners, and it was no wonder they chased us with garden rakes, one after me in particular, crying in great frustration, "Him young Charlie, him velly much tlouble!"

The old hands had countless stories of the early station days. Good cooks were hard to come by, and there was always one coming or going. They seldom lasted long, because the men were inveterate practical jokers, but one Chinese cook stayed on for many months. One day a curious head shepherd asked, "Ah Lee, how is it you stay on here, and put up with all these rough jokes and ragging from the men?"

Ah Lee smiled and looked down at his folded hands, "Him play no more tlicks on me, me no more pee in the soup!"

The example of a man who died before I was born has always been with me in the person of my great-grandfather James Chapman Smith. Past records of his courage, and foresight, and plain guts, have been an inspiration to me, together with the efforts of my own father, whose pioneering, though coming at a later date, yet showed the same essentials of grit and determination. Their example has played no small part in bolstering my flagging spirits when circumstances have seemed against me, sometimes through bad luck, often self-inflicted, and all too often choked in red tape.

Our early education was at the Tuapeka Mouth School. We five boys, riding to school after the milking chores were done and breakfast over, found plenty of scope for hilarity and horse-play, particularly with the unwelcome prospect of the evening chores and the milking of the house-cows ahead of us. One schoolboy neighbour found an ingenious way to save himself work: he inserted a straw into the duct of each teat after the early milking, allowing the milk to continue to drain away during the day. By evening the job was done for him. What his father said when he found out is not recorded.

Although I grew into an average-sized boy it did not seem likely at one time. When my mother first came back from the nursing home the Irish housekeeper, on seeing me, is supposed to have raised her hands in horror, saying with great finality, "Sure, an' he's sich a miserable skin-a-m'link, he's hardly worth the rearin', and we'd best put him in the creek with the pups!" Too-frequent litters of pups on the farm necessitated the unpleasant duty of disposal, and my arrival home coincided with yet another surplus supply. Kate in her wisdom apparently thought the creek was the place for me too.

At 16 I was sent as a boarder to Campbell House, at the Otago Boys' High School in Dunedin, where I spent a year in the lowest form. That was in 1931. I was so homesick and miserable that I begged my father to let me leave and come home. I made the most extravagant promises, saying I would "milk all the cows on the place". As milking cows was one of my pet aversions, probably the promises were quickly forgotten.

Dislike for milking cows must have started early because my father never lets me forget the time I threw the milk bucket at him. I was seven at the time, and busy milking one of our very quiet house-cows. She was never baled or leg-roped, and we just milked her in the open sitting on a milking stool beside her. This day she wouldn't stand, but kept moving on just as I had settled myself on my little stool, all ready for some steady milking. I had almost reached the end of my patience, when my father called out some well-meant advice. This was the last straw and I threw the milk bucket at him, yelling, "Milk your own bloody cows!"

We five boys must have frayed parental tempers at times. Events which in retrospect seem funny can't have been so at the time. I remember when my eldest brother, six years old and the proud owner of a new hatchet, hacked off the brand-new shaft of a visitor's gig. Then the family and guests, all unknowing, enjoyed the wonderful heat from the last load of wood which had been brought in by a more than usually willing small boy. One can imagine the consternation of my parents when the time came for their guests to depart.

After my brief sojourn at boarding-school, life became a round of farm chores. I liked doing things that required muscular effort, probably because I was smaller than my brothers, and had to put up with being called the "cull" of the family. About this time too, I fancied the idea of going to sea, although my main aim was to be an admiral: apparently I thought it was easier to start at the top and work my way down! With seafaring in mind I used to shin up and down ropes in the highest pine trees, and this helped me to develop a muscular torso, but to my disgust my legs never matched, and in later years these made me the target for rude comment when wearing drill shorts on active service.

Apart from these minor exertions there were hours and hours of tractor driving, sowing wheat, and other crops, and breaking in new ground at Cranleigh. In 1907 my father acquired 1,200 acres from the Clydevale estate and later he added 800 acres to it. It was here as we grew older that my brothers and I spent hours and hours of tractor driving, Clem and Dick especially, working round the clock. They even rigged up a caravan and had it parked near by so that they could work in shifts through the night, with just the big tractor lights to show the way immediately ahead.

Some of the Cranleigh boundaries were shared by farmers whose land extended up into the Blue Mountains, and there

B

seemed something about this isolated area that bred rugged individualists. Local gossip credited one settler with being a retired bushranger, and because he wouldn't send his children to school he was one day threatened with prosecution. During a local sale, at which he was present, a huge pall of smoke was seen – the school was on fire and was gutted. The authorities suspected arson and some plain-clothes detectives were sent into the district to make inquiries, but in order to cover their tracks they passed themselves off as miners panning for gold in the river. The suspect was known to be an excellent shot, and so when in quick succession three bullets thudded to the right, left, and a few inches behind the pseudo miners, they took the hint and left the district without delay, and no more was heard of the incident.

One boundary neighbour, an Irishman, had a somewhat perverse and contentious nature. He was always cross-grained. Late one March day my father in passing extended to him the compliments of the season, and he replied, "And I'll not be shaking hands with the likes of you, until ye've explained why you didn't say good-day to me that time last November the fourteenth, when I was foot-rottin' them ewes in your yards."

When my father protested mildly that he hadn't even seen him, he replied, "Well that doesn't matter, ye didn't say good-day!"

When this individualist passed away, somebody was heard to remark, "Och! well, there won't half be some bloody rows in heaven now!"

The Blue Mountains were part of our childhood. We looked there every morning for weather indications, people got lost in them, shot themselves there accidentally, or shot each other in mistake for a deer or wild pig. I liked to wander up there on my own, enjoying the solitude, observing the bird-life and flora and fauna, and sometimes deerstalking or pighunting. I sometimes tried to imagine the tension and defiance and hatred that had built up behind the closed doors of one isolated little homestead, where a settler had killed his daughter with an axe when she persisted in seeing the man she was courting against her father's wishes. After the deed he took to the bush, finally giving himself up to the police at Beaumont.

As I got older and in between daydreaming about going to sea or travelling the world, I was picker-up and rouseabout in the woolshed, milking the cows when I couldn't get out of it and generally, I suppose, looking for excitement and a change in the daily round.

Then the *Otago Daily Times* ran a flying competition, and this opened up an entirely new avenue of thought for me. The competitors had to take various tests, including a flight, and the successful candidate was to be given free tuition to acquire his A Licence. Needless to say I didn't win the contest, but it didn't stop me wanting to learn to fly.

Money was a problem of course, especially at this time, just after the Depression, when everybody was hard up. I borrowed a couple of horses and a grass-seed stripper from my father, and spent some weeks gathering browntop seed, which at that time was bringing about eight cents a pound. The seed was used extensively in the United States for sowing out golf greens, and also when crushed, as a preservative for smooth wooden surfaces such as wooden aircraft propellers.

With $140 saved, I went to Taieri and joined the Otago Aero Club, determined to stay there until I had got my A Licence. I found board with a delightful couple, Mr and Mrs White of Factory Road, Mosgiel, who were wonderful hosts to me.

The late Ted Olsen, a well known and popular figure in aviation, and a first-class pilot, was my instructor. During World War II as Air Commodore Olsen, he was one of the commanding officers of 75 NZ Squadron, but died of a serious illness just before the war ended.

My first solo landing was memorable – to me. Coming into land I found myself uncomfortably near the high-tension lines surrounding the airfield. To avoid them I put on motor and pulled the stick back, but in the resulting confusion I cut the

throttle and forgot to push the stick forward. There was a very
unpleasant "graunching" noise as the nose of the aircraft ground
into the earth just 18 in. over the fence. That was the shortest
bit of landing field I ever used.

The tail of the Gypsy Moth was pointing straight into the sky,
and from my vantage point, standing on the rudder pedals, I
could see my normally quite relaxed instructor jumping up and
down and shaking his fist. He wasted no time in getting me up
again. That Gypsy Moth ZK-ABF was the only aeroplane I
pranged during my flying career, with the exception of a
Hudson ground-looped at Whenuapai.

Attending the Club do's wasn't easy; home was 70 miles
away, and I was dependent on getting lifts with friends going the
same way. For a time club flying kept me satisfied, but it was
very time-consuming. Even flying the DH Moth at the Balclutha
Aero Club only 20 miles away could be disappointing; it meant
walking or cycling a round trip of 40 miles in the hope of 15
minutes' flying. Sometimes after arrival the weather would pack
up, and getting home in pelting rain or freezing snow or sleet
wasn't much fun.

About this time I put in an application to join the RNZAF
but was turned down on educational grounds, not even being
granted an interview. I was strongly advised against going to
London to join the RAF as in the authorities' opinion I wouldn't
stand a show; and furthermore, they said, having got there and
not been accepted I would be a liability on the country.

I wasn't particularly impressed by this advice, and having
accepted a job on the Shaw Savill ship *Fordsdale* sailed from Port
Chalmers on 28 January 1936, just six months after my 20th
birthday.

Fordsdale was a refrigerated cargo ship, and my time was spent
in chipping rust from the sides of the ship, and repainting the
patches, swabbing down decks, polishing brasswork, and helping in the galley.

So for a bob a month I worked my way to England and
opportunity.

2

The RAF takes a Gamble

I TRAVELLED straight up to London. We weren't due to be
signed off for a week, but as my pay had been only a bob a
month there was no point in hanging about waiting for it;
and anyway I had £2 in my pocket, enough to get me to the
Air Ministry for an interview.

My father had arranged an open account for me at the
National Mortgage Head Office, and I had a letter of introduction to Viscount Hampden, then Head of the London headquarters. I never used the letter, and only £50 of the account.
This saw me through from the time of my arrival in London
until I began training.

After arranging for an interview, I went to stay with an aunt
living near Ashford in Kent, spending several weeks there, helping in the garden, mowing lawns and pruning the roses, in
between getting my uncle off-side with my aunt, for taking me
to the local for a few pints. Then north to Scotland, and
chopping down trees in Perthshire. Back in London at the
approach of summer, but there was still no word from the Air
Ministry, so I spent a few weeks cherry-picking and harvesting
in Kent.

I had almost given up hope of the interview and had made
tentative arrangements to work my way to Texas on a cattle-
boat, when a letter came from Adastral House asking me to
report quite soon. I went to one of the fifty-bob tailors and
bought a new suit, but hurrying along the Strand, anxious not
to be late for my appointment, I was dive-bombed by a pigeon,
which rather sullied my sartorial perfection. Down in the men's
room of the underground station, a hurried attempt to remove

the mess only made it more obvious, but later I learnt that it was considered good luck to be so honoured by a Strand pigeon.

A panel of serious-looking gentlemen interviewed me, one with an enormous moustache and a twinkling eye, the others dour and forbidding. They asked me many questions. What school had I attended? Educational qualifications? Why had I had to work my way to England? Couldn't my father afford to send me? What did I know about algebra and geometry? What were my interests? Why did I want to join the RAF?

I bared my sketchy schooling to their critical gaze, and told them that my father could well afford to pay my fare to England, but that I'd preferred to get there in my own way. Algebra and geometry qualifications were pretty slim. As for my reasons for joining the RAF, I was ready for that one: I said I was interested in service life.

This was true anyway, and if my main reason was the desire to fly, I knew better than to tell it to my interrogators, as I'd been told that this was the surest way to prejudice an interview. After a few more questions, someone asked, "Do you drink?"

"Yes," I said. "I have a pint now and again."

The officer with the moustache suppressed a grin, and I was sent out into the corridor while they deliberated. It was a depressingly cold place, not improved by the sight of pale, intent-looking fellows dashing in and out of offices, clutching bundles of files tied up with red tape, obviously with the weight of the world on their shoulders.

"Anyway," I consoled myself. "I've still got the Texas job lined up."

Soon I was recalled. "Well, Lucas," they said, "we like your spirit, and we've decided to take a gamble on you. If you pass your medical test you can start your training right away."

Medically I was OK, but the dental standard was not so good, and I was required to produce a certificate proclaiming me dentally sound before I could start training. The dentist my aunt recommended had been a Royal Flying Corps pilot, and while he removed all my teeth he reminisced about his war

experiences with particular reference to ferrying the old
Maurice Farmans to France.

I was so interested that I hardly felt the extractions, and he,
knowing how the wheels grind exceeding slow at the Air
Ministry, gave me my certificate to post at once, assuring me
that by the time the reply came he would have me dentally fit.
Within a week he had me back in his surgery fitting the new
dentures, and next day the letter came, telling me to report to
Sywell, Northamptonshire, Elementary Flying School, which
was a civilian school run by Brooklands Aviation.

My days were filled with lectures and flying instruction,
during the three months *ab initio* training at Brooklands EFTS.

I had to try to forget all I'd learnt in civilian flying, and learn
the Air Force way. In fact the chaps who'd had no flying experience at all seemed to get on faster than those of us who had
rudimentary knowledge. It was a lot of fun, however, and not
too difficult.

Our instructor, "Sailor" Hayward, must have suffered at
times. I remember him trying to teach me to do slow rolls, and
I was darned if I could do them; I just fell out of the sky instead.
When he couldn't stand it any longer he landed, taxied over to
the hangar and got out.

I started to follow, but he turned and snarled, "No bloody
fear you don't. You can stay right there. Get up and stay over
that wood at 2,000 ft and practise slow rolls until you can do
them!"

Still smarting from his tone of voice and my own incompe-
tence, I climbed to 2,500 ft, smoothing my ruffled feelings with
the thought that the petrol supply of the Tiger Moth was not in-
exhaustible; come down some time I must, whether I had mastered
his bloody slow rolls or not. After cruising round for a while I
finally scraped up the nerve to give it a go. I got up to the required speed, pulled up the nose, pushed the stick over, and the
machine went on its back, and this was the moment when all I
had ever learnt about slow rolls vanished from my mind.

I hung upside down in the straps wondering, "What the hell

do I do now?", trying to dredge up from memory every little thing I had been taught. I got out of it by pulling the stick back and coming out as if in a loop. Well, I was still in one piece, and getting the feel of the aeroplane, so climbed again for another try, and after several more attempts felt I'd mastered the business well enough to face my instructor again, and was mildly surprised to find him recovering from an attack of nerves. However, slow rolls held no more fears for me from that day, and the three-months' course was soon over.

From Sywell we were sent down to Uxbridge for a disciplinary course. We were a pretty mixed lot in those early training days. There was a confusion of Welsh, English, Irish, Scots, and Canadians, Rhodesians and South Africans, besides Americans and New Zealanders. I don't remember any Australians in our course although there were several in the next.

We were always borrowing from one another. Pay for acting-pilot officers on probation, temporary, unpaid, was not generous, and the 14s. a day did not stretch far. We rose daily at 6 a.m. with physical training and ablutions before breakfast and square-bashing until midday. The rest of the time was taken up with lectures.

Still in civilian clothes, we were a bunch of weird-looking types sporting pork-pie hats, like North Canterbury farmers, old grey bags and sports jackets, with peculiar hair-styles and some eye-catching moustaches.

Afternoon leave was given to go to London to be fitted for uniforms. I went to Gieves of Old Bond Street, who are service tailors, well known to generations of servicemen and women, with a reputation for efficiency and personal service. I bought my first uniform in 1936, and in 1943 they still remembered my name and measurements.

We were all terribly keen, very proud of our uniforms, and of being one of the team. Just before the end of the course we were paraded in full uniform, without wings, before the Commanding Officer. He gave us a pep talk in traditional style, designed to knock back any signs of swelled heads, concluding on a typical

note: "Just because you chaps have your uniforms, don't think
you're anybody – because you're not. You're just the lowest
form of animal life!"

I often wonder what our CO would have said about low
animal life if he had observed my occasional "toothabatics" at
parties in the mess; when suitably in the mood I'd show the
boys how to rotate false teeth without removing them from my
mouth. Once when I did this someone called out "Popeye" –
chiefly I think because my jaw jutted out during my performance. Anyway, the name stuck – so much so that one night
later on and unknown to me till I walked out on to the tarmac,
an artist among the groundcrew painted a very lifelike Popeye
character on my aircraft. I've been known as Popeye ever since.

January 1937 found us at No 10 Flying Training School at
Ternhill, Shropshire, for a three-months' training course to be
followed by a fortnight's leave, and then another three months
at Advanced Training School. By this time we had graduated to
a more advanced type of aircraft, the Hawker Hart and Hawker
Audax, with Rolls-Royce Kestrel motors. Advanced training
was completed in August 1937, and my posting came for No 10
Squadron, No 4 Bomber Group, at Dishforth in Yorkshire,
where "Bomber" Harris was Air Officer Commanding.

My friend Stew Young and I were the only two out of our
course to be posted there, and we set out for Dishforth by bus
from York via Boroughbridge. Bearing in mind the earlier
advice about feeling our way into a new squadron, we were
walking sedately up to the mess when an old "bomb" came
careering round the corner. The officers were having a competition to see who could drive an old Morris Minor the fastest
around the mess. The contest came to a halt when the wire
wheels buckled. It was then I met the owner of the car, Aubrey
Breckon, who on finding I was a fellow New Zealander invited
me to go with him into Boroughbridge to have the car repaired,
and a couple at the local while we waited. After the war Breck
retired from the RNZAF with the rank of group captain and a

DFC, and is now Management Liaison Officer with Air New Zealand.

To Stew and me the Whitleys looked enormous after the little training machines we were used to, and we wondered how we would ever learn to master them. But they were no trouble after all and in a day or two we were taking them for granted. I flew Whitleys from August 1937 until July 1939, and it was while flying one that I went on my first long, night cross-country training flight, in order to be classified as a captain.

Two of us were detailed for this and my opposite number, Dusty Miller, took off and set course, but precisely in the opposite direction. Everything went smoothly until I changed course at Dungeness to fly north to Newcastle, where I struck thick cloud and icing conditions. These were the days before blind-flying panels had been installed, but at last I obtained a fix from our base which placed me 80 miles off-course and over the North Sea. I changed course for Yorkshire, but the air-speed indicator had iced up and I could judge my speed only by the noise of the engines. We became so heavily iced-up that it was all I could do to maintain height, periodically scraping ice off the compass bowl to check my course.

One and a half hours later I flew out of cloud to find visibility good for miles. With relief I could see the Dishforth beacon flashing and the flarepath twinkling about two miles off my starboard bow. Two hours after the Whitley had been hangared ice was still falling off the wings. I wondered how long the other aircraft had been in before me, but was told that nothing had been heard from him. He vanished without trace; it was assumed that instead of going above cloud, as I had done, to avoid icing conditions, that he had gone below for the same reasons and that in doing so his plane had become so heavily iced-up that the controls froze, forcing him into the North Sea.

In September 1938 our squadron went to Evanton, near Invergordon in the north of Scotland, for the annual bombing and air-firing practice camp, dropping bombs off the coast, and doing air-firing practice on drogues and ground targets, with machine guns set up in the turrets.

While we were there the Munich crisis occurred, and the night before Mr Chamberlain flew to Germany the Home Fleet filled the Cromarty Firth. One could hardly see the water for ships – aircraft carriers, battleships, cruisers, tenders, and submarines. The next morning there was hardly a ripple on the water, and of the thousands of tons of shipping not a sign. For the first time I really understood how the Navy got the name the "Silent Service".

A few days later we were all immensely relieved to hear that war had been staved off, as our defences were in pretty poor shape. The scare, however, sharply focused attention on the general lack of preparedness and defence facilities. The Whitleys had little in the way of armament, and in order to provide some fire-power, holes were cut in the fuselage and Lewis guns installed.

Back at Dishforth training continued, heightened by the threat of war. In this year too I married Joan Chapman Smith, a cousin from New Zealand.

In July 1939 we were shifted to Marham in Norfolk where a New Zealand Flight was being formed. The New Zealand Government was re-equipping its Air Force with an anticipated 30 Wellington bombers, and it asked New Zealanders serving in the RAF to transfer to the RNZAF in order to ferry the first six Wellingtons out to New Zealand. I was one of 12 chosen. In anticipation of this flight my wife left by ship for home. The date for my departure from the UK was set for October. But war intervened: I was just sewing on my Flying Officer's stripe when the Prime Minister announced over the air that we were at war with Germany.

3

A Taste of War

ON THE FIRST DAY of the war 24 aircraft from Bomber Command were sent on a daylight raid to Wilhelmshaven, and of a number sent from our station, only one returned. In those early raids losses were high, and the enemy seemed to have fairly reliable advance notice of our movements.

In October 1939 the New Zealand Flight, as we now were, went to Harwell Operational Training Unit in Berkshire to familiarise ourselves with the Wellingtons. The late Air Commodore Maurice Buckley, CBE, then a squadron leader was our commanding officer and taught us to fly them, and our navigators and air-gunners took a course at the same time.

For a time our future was uncertain. At first the NZ Flight was to be disbanded, and its members posted to RAF squadrons, but the Chief of Bomber Command, Air Marshal Sir Charles Portal, thought that the New Zealanders should be kept as a separate unit within his command. Thus we were able to keep our identity throughout the war.

It took time to bring the Wellingtons up to operational standard. They had been stripped of all their war equipment in readiness for the 13,000-mile flight to New Zealand, and all this had to be replaced and numerous modifications made for better defence. My first operational flight with the NZ Squadron as it was now known was made on 13 March 1940, when we did a sweep looking for enemy shipping in the North Sea. Then on 6 April I had to drop some of those confounded leaflets and false ration cards over Nienburg, Petershagen, and Steinhudermeer.

On 17 April I flew as second pilot with John Collins of Christchurch, to attack an aerodrome at Stavanger in Norway. John later went missing after taking part in a sortie over Dinant. He was the Squadron's first casualty. After more of these abortive raids, dropping bits of paper and getting shot at for our pains, we got into the real thing once the Germans pressed on with their invasion of the Netherlands and Belgium.

By May 1940 the Air Ministry had officially announced that we were to be known as No 75 NZ Squadron, and we at last had our proper place in the hierarchy. By this time we had moved from Harwell to Stradishall, then, on 16 February finally to Feltwell, in East Anglia, which was to become our base.

My first op over Germany proper was on 21 May when we bombed the railway marshalling-yards at Aachen. After that we were bombing night after night, behind the lines; we started fires and explosions in woods and during troop concentrations right up to the time of Dunkirk, and we were still bombing on that last night.

The Air Force was accused at the time of not giving proper cover to the Army at Dunkirk but little did the chaps on the ground know that we were there all right – only there weren't enough of us.

Then we started on Germany itself, bombing oil refineries and poison gas factories. After a raid on Leverkusen in Köln, our Intelligence reported that 2,000 of the inhabitants and employees in the area had been shifted to the Austrian Tyrol to recuperate from the poison gas fumes. Bremen, Hamburg, Kiel, Düsseldorf, Cologne, Emden, Lübeck, Kassel, and Gotha, will always live in the memories of the Allied air forces of our generation. Hamm and Soest, great ganglions of marshalling-yards, covering over $1\frac{1}{2}$ square miles, the nerve centres of the German railway system often packed with trucks and trains, took terrific punishment. Acting upon intelligence reports, we bombed the Black Forest to destroy the build-up of arms dumps and stores reported hidden there.

Setting fire to crops was another job inspired by the back-room boys; phosphorus pills and pieces of cellulose kept soaking in containers of liquid were tipped down the flare chute over the German wheat belt. If it was a fine day they would ignite as the sun dried them out.

Bombs were set for a 30-minute to a 72-hour delay. One never knew when these things were about to explode, so while flying back to England, or even when safe in bed, they could still be going off, hampering reclamation efforts by the enemy. The colossal fires caused by the bombing of fuel plants staggered the imagination, and a direct hit on a target left us feeling utterly naked and exposed. The billowing smoke and flame lit up the area for miles and up to a height of 7,000 or 8,000 ft, which was about the limit for Wellingtons then. In the Marks IA and IC it took all our time, right from Feltwell in England to the Dutch coast, to climb to 8,000 ft, and even so, the cylinder-head temperature would be very high. Once the bombs were away more height could be gained, but we needed it more going in.

Summer nights were short, and a trip to Bremen then meant a daylight take-off and formating until dark. By this time the German coast would be just below, and from then on we were on our own. Getting back across the coast before sun-up had its moments: on a clear morning we were a sitting duck for enemy fighters.

In the early 1940s when searchlights were operated by sound locators, our air-gunners made a nick in the tail of a 4-lb incendiary bomb, causing it to whistle in its descent in imitation of a full-size bomb. Momentarily the searchlights would go out, presumably while the crews dived for cover, and with luck we'd have nipped past the danger zone. De-synchronising the engines succeeded for a while, as also falling champagne bottles. Later on these devices didn't work, as both sides became more sophisticated in the use of radar.

As time went on there became established a solid 20-mile belt of searchlights. Once we had crossed the German and Dutch coasts master searchlights, operated by radar, might pick up the aircraft; the others would then home-in to fix the intruder in a solid cone of light. When pinpointed, and if no flak was about, we could be sure that the enemy were holding off to allow their night fighters to come in for the kill. It was a helpless feeling; we knew there were big concentrations of fighters stationed round the searchlight belt, just waiting for us, apart from others lying in wait farther on, guarding targets we might be heading for. Being caught in the cone could be, and often was, fatal.

We soon learned that it wasn't much use to weave and dodge, to evade the light; but I would throttle back, stick the nose down, and with eyes glued to the instrument panel, watch the altimeter unwinding at a fantastic speed. To look outside was to be instantly blinded by glare; meanwhile, the front gunner would be spraying the searchlights with machine-gun fire, and although our height made the fire mostly ineffectual, the tracer would often demoralise the enemy enough to make him douse the lights for a few seconds. At 5,000 ft I'd pull-out gradually because of the bombs aboard – then open to full throttle, and start the long climb again, with fingers crossed, hoping we were safely through the belt.

After 30 ops my tour was nearly over, but I heard on the grapevine that the first-ever trip to Berlin was coming off soon. Goering was still boasting that enemy aircraft would never fly over the capital of the Third Reich, and this was to be the RAF's answer to his boast. I pressed our CO, Wing Commander Buckley, to let me stay on until then, and after some hesitation he okayed it, as the raid was planned for the following night.

Next day all the crews not required went on leave, but shortly after briefing-time we found that the target had been changed, and I did six more trips before Berlin came up. It was 23 September 1940. The night was perfect, spoilt only by continuous flak all the way there and back. Over Berlin things warmed up considerably, and on such a clear night we had no trouble in picking out our target, nor indeed did the enemy. Everything was clear-cut – waterways, railways, autobahns, and our target, the Tempelhof railway station. Besides the flashes of fire and the smoke from our own bombs, we were bucketed about quite severely by flak, both there and on the way home, but apparently not hit.

Home base was fogged up, and we had to go on to Marham, where on landing we did a Waltzing Matilda down the flare-path, in and out of the flares, to finish up near the second last one with no further damage, except a drunken lean which made the aircraft look like a gigantic crippled bird. A piece of shrapnel had sliced a huge hunk out of one of the tyres.

During these days everybody was under tension. After the long night raids were over and de-briefing concluded, we would drift off to bed, having eaten the usual bacon and two eggs, special fare for those returning from ops, and fall asleep to peace on earth, the sun shining, the birds singing, and all the sounds of early morning. The previous hours of darkness receded like some fantastic dream.

I suppose the relaxation after a few hours' sleep, particularly if we were not scheduled for another trip that night, acted like a stimulant, and it didn't take much to get us in the mood for a bit of nonsense in the mess. After one such night I found I'd "walked the ceiling", making a path of black footprints across the anteroom ceiling, down a wall, and out through a ventilator. This effort was performed in an atmosphere of great hilarity and enthusiasm. By the time we'd had a few beers the chaps were ready for anything, and whether I was stripped or did it volun-tarily, I was soon down to my jockeys, spread-eagled on one of the enormous chesterfields, while someone industriously blackened the soles of my feet with shoe polish.

Not long after, Air Chief Marshal Sir Arthur Tedder, later Lord Tedder, visited the station and wrote in the Visitors' Book, "These footprints to remain for all time!", thus putting the seal of official approval on a prank that had been frowned on in some quarters.

The Berlin raid marked my 37th op and the end of my first tour.

I spent the next six months at Hampstead Norris, a Welling-ton Operational Training Unit, and a satellite of Harwell. Posted here for conversion to bombers were New Zealanders who had been training in Canada and Australian, Rhodesian, Canadian, and British pilots. Training went on night and day, regardless of the constant raids on London not far away.

The weather was cold and wet, the grassed areas of the aerodrome always a morass. The tar-sealed runways crumbled at the edges if one taxied too close, and it was all too easy to get bogged. One night I was standing in gumboots, ankle-deep in mud, by an old farm barn which did temporary duty as our office. I had just sent a pupil solo and was watching him coming in to land.

Someone said, "What the hell's that Blenheim doing flying low over there?"

It was a moonlight night, and London was in the middle of an air-raid. Searchlights were criss-crossing the night sky, and everywhere there was an eerie glow from fires and flak. For a Blenheim he was pretty unfriendly; he laid a stick of bombs right across "Piccadilly Circus" – the intersection of the runways. The bombs skipped off into the grass, and the Ju88, for that was what it was, disappeared, while my pupil, quite unperturbed, came into land unaware of the incident and intent only on making a good landing.

While at Hampstead Norris I was summoned to Buckingham Palace to receive the DFC from the late King George VI, and found there on a similar mission the late Squadron Leader W. M. C. Williams, a son of the late Canon W. C. Williams of Napier. We were the only New Zealanders at the investiture, and this had reached the notice of the King. He spoke to me for several moments, asking questions about New Zealand, how long had I been in England, and so on, then shook my hand and, smiling, expressed the hope that he'd see me back again. Bill Williams was similarly singled out.

At the end of my six months at Hampstead Norris I managed to get back to Feltwell, and was fortunate in getting back some of my old crew, wireless operator Sgt Gould, Sgt Navigator Green, both of whom received their DFMs with me on my first tour, and my old air-gunner Sgt Fenton.

c

During the months I had been away from operational flying, scientific development in the promotion of the war had gone ahead, especially in radar and anti-aircraft practices. In the mess we discussed safe heights for bombing. Somebody said that 20,000 ft was the safest. During my first tour we had always flown at between 7,000 and 8,000 ft, and thinking of the extreme cold at 20,000 ft I decided to stay at the height I'd been used to.

Our first target was Dusseldorf, and I flew at 8,000 ft. Over the target the navigator said that the aircraft wasn't quite steady enough – we were getting thrown about a bit by flak – and would I please go around again. We were getting all hell pasted out of us, but we made another run-in. Still this wasn't good enough for our navigator, and so back we went again. By this time all we were interested in was getting home to Mum. It was a bit frightening up there, waiting for anything to happen, watching the instruments, concentrating on them, trying not to notice the birthday celebrations outside, with shell-flashes and tracer zipping past and searchlights feeling for us everywhere.

It must have been an absorbing pastime for the navigator lying there on his belly, watching what was being thrown up from below. On the last run-in there was an almighty *whang*. Luckily the bombs were gone, for our hydraulics were shot away, the bomb-doors wouldn't close, and the undercart fell down. One motor had been hit and started a small fire, which fortunately went out. The petrol tanks were holed. Leaning forward to set the gyro compass, I heard a swishing noise behind my head: shrapnel as big as a fist had come in one window and crashed out the other, slicing through the air where my neck had been seconds before.

I felt a pluck at my sleeve, and turned around, but found no one there. It was another piece of shrapnel that had penetrated the sleeve of my overall and passed on, not even tearing the uniform sleeve beneath. We turned back through all this lot, gradually losing height, and with the petrol gauge going down alarmingly. At the Dutch coast we were down to 200 ft. Should we ditch and then try to escape capture, or give it a go across the

Channel and home to Mum? Give it a go, said the crew; so we headed out across the North Sea, just managing to hold our height at 200 ft. Our ETA for the East Anglian coast was up and, sure enough, I thought, there's the coast; but no, it was just a cloud shadow on the water. Petrol was really low now, and the port motor was barely ticking over. The cylinder-head temperature was right off the clock, almost at melting-point, but the other motor was still running sweetly. At last the coast was below and then behind us, and though we were near our home base we were refused permission to land there because of un-exploded bombs on the airfield from a German raid.

Now, with only 100 ft of height, we had to get to Newmarket, 15 miles away, with petrol so low that every time I canted a wing to do a turn the motor cut. At Newmarket Control held us off as a Stirling had priority, but we had to go in regardless. We managed to get the undercart pumped down by hand, and I put the Wellington down in the dark, well away to the right of the flarepath. She floated for ages, and the tanks were so empty that just as we touched down the one remaining motor cut.

Tim Williams, from Hawke's Bay, was my second pilot, and this was his first trip. While we were all lying under the wing waiting for transport he remarked, "Gee! if all the trips are like this one, it won't be so bad."

It was one of the worst I'd ever had, and I told him what he could do with them. We were lying there on our parachutes, waiting for the truck to come, in blessed silence and the peace was terrific. All the aircraft that would ever return were back, and only someone who had looked death in the face could have understood what these few quiescent moments meant to us.

It was during these moments that we thought of the others who never came back – brave men such as Sgt Pilot Jimmy Ward, of Wanganui, who never returned from a raid I had sent him on to Hamburg. Just before that, Jimmy Ward had won New Zealand's first VC of the war by his daring feat on a Wellington 13,000 ft up. He had climbed out on to the starboard wing to put out a fire which threatened to destroy the aircraft.

His crew mate, Sgt Observer L. A. Lawton, of Wellington, shared in this magnificent display of courage by risking his life to pull Jimmy back into the Wellington.

The next op was Düsseldorf again, and almost a repeat performance, so the following trip saw us flying at a height of 20,000 ft frozen stiff. Far below a Wellington was silhouetted on top of a black cloud, with puffs all around it.

I thought smugly, "You silly ass, you should be up here where it's safe."

At that moment there was an appalling crash as a shell exploded directly beneath us. "To hell with this," I thought, "I'm not going to be shot at *and* frozen stiff as well." So we dropped down to 8,000 ft again and finished the tour at this height.

On one mission, as we were getting near the English coast at Felixstowe, near Harwich, we were fired at quite a lot by our own guns, and I asked my navigator to fire the colours of the day from the Very pistol. He'd no sooner placed the cartridge than the firing stopped. So the pistol was temporarily pushed into the parachute stowage while we continued on to base.

Next day when I came back on station I found my aircraft, which I'd left two miles away in a revetment, standing burnt out on the tarmac. I was greatly puzzled, but on inquiry found that the armourer, new to the job, who'd inspected the ancillary equipment had an altogether novel way of testing the Very pistol. He had pulled the trigger; unfortunately, the gun was pointing straight at the radio set. It had been quite a spectacular blaze.

This was just the start of the trouble. Group Captain Buckley called me to his office. He was a wonderful fellow, a real father to us boys. He had taught me to fly Wellingtons, he had been my flight commander and squadron commander, and was now my station commander. Later on he was to be my AOC (Air Officer Commanding our Group). Now he was greatly concerned over this mishap to my aircraft, for he'd received word that we had to report to the AOC, Air Vice-Marshal Baldwin, an officer who did a tremendous amount for New Zealanders. In fact, nobody could have done more for us in No 3 Group.

I had to go on the mat at 1500 hours next day to explain the accident. By this time I was feeling really apprehensive. When I came face to face with the Air Vice-Marshal he said, "I hope you realise the seriousness of this, Lucas?"

"Yes, sir. I do, sir."

"Have you read Bomber Command Orders?"

"Yes, sir."

"Then you know that it is the captain's responsibility to see that all guns are unloaded before leaving the aircraft?"

"Yes, sir." I knew this quite well, but it was one of the standing orders more honoured in the breach. Still, ultimately the responsibility was mine.

"This is so serious," he went on, "and we're so short of aircraft, that I shall have to make an example of this. Everybody must be made fully aware of their responsibilities."

My knees were really knocking now, but the stern voice continued, "Mind you, I might well have done the same thing myself, but that's not the point. How do you want this dealt with? By me, or by court martial?"

At the mention of court martial all sorts of visions flashed through my mind, and I saw myself returned to New Zealand in disgrace.

"By you, sir," I said in a shaky voice.

"Very well. You are admonished."

I was much more careful after that.

On 26 November 1941 I carried my first 4,000-lb bomb, and the target was Emden. We were flying a Mark IV Wellington with Rolls-Royce Merlin engines, and the bomb, looking like a couple of 44-gallon drums joined together, actually descended below the fuselage, so that the bomb-doors couldn't quite close.

The late King Paul of Greece, then Crown Prince, was visiting the station, and he came out to see the aircraft, getting down on his hands and knees to pat the bomb protruding from its belly.

He said he'd like to be on hand when we got back, and silently I thanked him for his faith on our return.

Once over the target, and with the bomb away, we cruised at 10,000 ft waiting to see the effect. Just as we began to think we'd dropped a dud, the aircraft rocked with a colossal explosion and a ring of fire kept on spreading, with the force of the blast, for about 40 seconds. It was in the early hours of the morning when we got back, but the Crown Prince was waiting, and he came down with us to the de-briefing-room to hear our account of the trip. He was being shown around by a naval brass-hat who was also an old school friend of his, and they came along with me to the mess for our traditional two eggs and a mug of beer.

I was a little out of my depth when they spoke animatedly of former schooldays. The Naval officer asked the Crown Prince what had happened to old So-and-so, and the Crown Prince replied, "Oh, he's done very well, he's the duke of somewhere." Or about someone else: "He's the king of someplace."

This was a long way from my schooldays in New Zealand, so I carried on with my beer and eggs, and tried to stop my ears flapping.

I saw them off in their staff car and got a kick out of the Crown Prince's invitation, "Pop up to the Palace, Popeye, any time you're in Athens." It was a pleasant interlude, and he was a charming person. I never did get a chance to pop up to the Palace but I always followed his career with interest.

In 1940 my wife, Joan, had come back to England after the birth of our daughter and we'd been living off-station in a rented house in Lakenheath village. The blitz was at its height, and night-bombing was fairly heavy round our area at Feltwell. I was getting back in the dawn hours after night after night of operations; during this time my wife died suddenly in her sleep. She was given a military funeral and buried in the Services section in St Mary's Churchyard at Feltwell.

4

Home Again

AFTER COMPLETING MY SECOND TOUR of operations I was posted to a Blind Approach Training School at Swindon where, if the morning was soggy and foggy and visibility only half-way across the aerodrome, it was considered perfect flying weather.

Returning to Feltwell, I commanded No 1519 BAT (Blind Approach Training) Flight for a short while before being posted back to New Zealand in March 1942, with some other New Zealanders. After the fall of Pearl Harbour and with the threat of further Japanese aggression in the Pacific we were being sent home in the quickest way possible.

We left in what was said to be one of the biggest troop convoys ever to have left Britain. There wasn't a troopship under 15,000 tons, and we were escorted by the aircraft carrier *Illustrious* and the battleship *Malaya*, 10 destroyers, and four or five armed merchant cruisers, all responsible for the safety of well over half a million tons of merchant shipping. Our ship, the *Dominion Monarch*, had been only partially converted for troop-carrying, and still had good china and cutlery, splendid meals, and well-stocked bars.

We zigzagged our way from Liverpool to Sierra Leone and then on to Cape Town, then Bombay. When our ship berthed at Sydney we learnt that the wives and children of some of the officers who had been embarked on a so-called "slow" freighter some three weeks after our departure from England were already in New Zealand. So much for our "fast" trip home. They had steamed straight through from London to Panama in an old cargo ship with no rails or safeguards to keep small children and toddlers from falling overboard. They'd had no convoy protection and cabin space for only 12, but the captain and crew had been kindness itself.

Among the passengers were the wives of Squadron Leaders Garry Kain and the late W. M. C. Williams, with their small sons and my two-year-old daughter, Wendy. Mrs Patsy Kain had offered to bring her out to the care of my parents in South Otago; she and the late Mrs Penny Williams had looked after Wendy and their own children in particularly trying conditions.

We sailed into Sydney on the morning after midget Japanese submarines had been sighted in the harbour and shelled by the Americans. It was here that I picked up an old *Weekly News* in the NZ Government Tourist Bureau, and saw that I had been awarded a bar to my DFC.

On arrival in New Zealand I applied for leave to a senior officer who had never seen overseas service. He was pettishly reluctant to grant my request. "Don't you know there's a *war* on?" he said accusingly. However I got my leave, and saw my family. It had been a worrying time getting a motherless baby properly looked after while I was on active service, and I shall always be grateful to the kind women who took care of her until I was posted back to New Zealand.

Back from leave I was supposed to initiate the installation of a blind approach landing system, and start a blind approach training flight in New Zealand, but this wasn't possible, as all the equipment had been sunk in transit. My next posting then was to Whenuapai, in command of No 1 General Reconnaissance Squadron. Apart from general submarine patrol, we did more fighter affiliation with the Kittyhawk squadrons than anything else.

One night we had a party in the mess, and the next morning there were footprints on the ceiling. Not long after this Sir Cyril Newall, then Governor-General, was scheduled to visit the station, and somebody in authority who thought the footprints in the mess were in bad taste had them removed.

The first thing the Governor asked to see when he walked into the mess were the footprints on the ceiling. He had to be told that they had been removed.

"What a pity!" he remarked. "It showed a fine spirit!"

We wasted no time, after His Excellency left, putting them right back again. The only other time I offended in this way in New Zealand was when I was leaving the Air Force. The sergeants carried me by force to their mess, where I had to put up my footprints emerging out of a flak burst painted on the ceiling, while two powerful sergeants held me up and saw that the job was done properly.

Then one Saturday night I smashed up my car in an unexpected introduction to a stationary tram, and after I was discharged from hospital was sent on leave to recuperate.

The next posting was again to Whenuapai, this time to form New Zealand's first air transport unit, No 40 Squadron. There was no aeroplane with which to start the initial service, and I spent a short time kicking my heels with nothing to do. Then one morning there appeared, parked on the tarmac in lonely splendour, a brand new DC3, the first to come to New Zealand.

Nobody seemed to be around to officially hand the aeroplane over, but the pilot's handbook lay open on the pilot's seat. I picked it up and sat studying it, matching up the knobs and switches with the diagrams, and getting the feel of the instrument panel. After a while I started up the motors, let the brakes off, and taxied a little. Everything seemed OK, so I phoned Squadron Leader Bill Tacon, CO of No 1 Squadron, who later as Wing Commander Tacon, DSO, DFC and bar, AFC, was to become Commander of the King's Flight, and personal pilot to His Majesty King George VI. I asked him to come along to act as "second dicky" for me while I tried some taxiing to see how she handled, and the next moment we were at the end of the runway and into wind, then I opened the throttles and we were airborne.

We cruised around, tried the radio and radio compass and all the other equipment, just as the book said.

Coming in to land, however, something was wrong. The undercart wouldn't lock down; instead, the warning horn kept blaring like a demented banshee, and the red danger light stayed on. This was somewhat unnerving and not quite according to Hoyle, so we made another circuit while we studied the handbook again, trying to fathom out the fault.

The book said: "In such circumstances such as this, if the hydraulic pressure is at a certain level, it is permissible to land." Well the pressure was OK, so we lined up on the runway and prepared to land. I never saw anybody move as fast as Bill did. He was down the fuselage and out of the door jamming in the two locking pins in a matter of seconds. I saw the fire-tender and station ambulance going back to their stations, and realised that there had been an alert for the possible crash-landing of our first and only Dakota. (The cause of the emergency was a faulty contact; when the undercarriage was down the contact points were by-passing one another.)

I did a 13-hour familiarisation flight around New Zealand next day, and on the day following Major Ross of the US Marine Corps arrived in New Zealand to check me out on the DC3 as it was then called. The DC3 was the civilian version, the Army called theirs a C47, the Navy an R4DI, and the RAF knew theirs as a Dakota – but they were all the same aeroplane. Major Ross didn't know that I'd already flown the aircraft around New Zealand, and nobody told him. Fifteen thousand hours on Dakotas, flying for a civilian airline in the USA, added up to a very experienced man, and I wanted to learn all I could from him.

Checking out on night-flying had its moments. I had been used to severe blackout conditions in England, with only the use of glim lamps which were not visible until the aircraft was lined up on the runway at about 500 ft. I wasn't used to the more liberal illumination practised in New Zealand. As I came in to land after the first circuit the Major was quite upset when I did not put on my landing lights, or request Control for the Chance

Light. It wasn't a bad landing, but he said, "The next time, boy, I guess we'll have some lights!"

So the next time around we called up for the whole works, and the place was lit up like a Christmas tree.

Coming in I bounced all over the runway. "Guess you don't need those lights after all!" he said resignedly.

A week later the Dakota's first official flight as No 40 Squadron was made. The date was 13 April 1943, and the destination Espiritu Santo, New Hebrides, then return. My crew were the late Lloyd Parry, then Flying Officer, as co-pilot, and Flying Officer Doug Newall, DFC, who had been navigational leader in one of the first Stirling raids on Italy. An MSc, he is now agricultural science master at Waitaki Boys' High School, and my sons, who are boarders there, see quite a lot of him. Doug was an extraordinarily fine navigator; he always got us exactly where we wanted to go regardless of weather. On the long hops from Espiritu Santo to Whenuapai his ability to bring us in dead on Waipapakauri had some of our American passengers almost believing in the supernatural.

Fred Mayer, our Flight Engineer, was another top man who had things really taped. Once when we were taking off from Fiji, heading north to Canton Island, smoke started to pour out from behind the switch panel; Fred had that panel off in no time and the wire disconnected. He burnt his hands, but without his quick thinking I don't know what sort of predicament we might have found ourselves in. Flight Sergeant Robbie Robson, who had just finished a Forward Pacific Area tour as wireless operator, made up the rest of this first crew.

Later Phil Le Couteur, then Flying Officer but now one of the senior captains of Air New Zealand's DC8s, became my second pilot. We logged some solid flying times in the next six months and were a pretty happy crew.

Soon we were settled down to a regular practice and became maid-of-all-work to the forward areas. The usual routine would be an 0600 hours, Monday morning take-off from Whenuapai,

on a direct course to the New Hebrides; then next morning on
to Guadalcanal, where sometimes we would have to stooge
around waiting for an artillery barrage and fighting around the
airstrip to clear before we could go in to land. We never made
any bones about unloading and loading up again fast and
getting the hell out of there, back to the New Hebrides, as with
no armament we felt pretty vulnerable. At 2100 hours on
Tuesday night we would leave the New Hebrides and fly
through the night to be back at Whenuapai for breakfast on
Wednesday morning. Thursday would see us off in the Lodestar
to Norfolk Island with the mail, and return to Whenuapai.
Friday at 0600 hours again, flying all day to Fiji and back all
night to Whenuapai, arriving for breakfast again on Saturday
morning. Next Monday we would start all over again.

The longest trip took 100 hours flying in one week. We flew
from Whenuapai to Fiji, then to Canton Island, Palmyra, and
Honolulu, carrying ferry crews who had been briefed to bring
back PVIs (Venturas). After a day at Honolulu we ferried some
American Navy flying-boat crews down to Palmyra and Canton, and across to Funafuti and Guadalcanal. Then we pushed
on down to the New Hebrides, across to Fiji, then back to
Honolulu, before returning to Whenuapai via Fiji.

Our principal task was to pioneer the best transport routes in
the area. We had to check prevailing weather conditions and
radio navigational aids, and note any other relevant factors
which would help to ensure a safe and regular run. The main
work was freighting goods and mail but we carried a diversity of
other items. The capacity of the Dak allowed about 5,000 lb of
freight or about 20 passengers. There were no frills or fancy
seating arrangements, and it depended on individual weights
just how many passengers we could carry, or what weight
margin was left for the freight.

We flew groundcrews to forward areas, and aircrews to ferry
aircraft back. We had as passengers VIPs and urgent sick cases,
men on sick or compassionate leave, or with psychiatric
troubles. The Dakota had a big wide cargo hatch, ideal for the

speedy loading and unloading of freight. We carried concrete-mixers, vegetables, aircraft parts and engines, drugs and jungle-kits, sly-grog, and hens, dead and alive. There was Christmas cheer, and letters by hand, and on the return trips, notes and messages, and phone calls to deliver or pass on. The smuggled washing-machines and other illicit traffic didn't always escape the watchful eye of the inspectors, but the boys always thought it worth a try, I suppose.

Always when we were flying up to the forward areas we made a point of filling up all spare space with mutton, or eggs and green vegetables. These items were some of the most missed by the troops. We would check the load sheet, note any space left, and then ring the ration sergeant to see what he could let us have to take forward for a change of diet. The men were sorely in need of fresh greens, and fruit in particular, although while the Americans were there, our boys were able to buy a certain amount from the American PX stores to vary the menu. Anything useful would go, including some crates of "brown bomber beer".

On 20 April 1943, during all this hurrying back and forth between New Zealand and the Pacific theatre, I married Loraine (Lorie) Flansburgh-Washbourne of Auckland, who was a member of the WAAF stationed at Whenuapai, driving transports and ambulances. It was a very short engagement as I was expecting, or hoping anyway, to be posted back to England for another tour of ops.

Getting approval for the posting took longer than I expected, and it was only after writing what I now consider in my more mellow years to have been a rather provocative letter that I got results. In it I said that my training as a night-bomber pilot was being wasted when trained personnel were still so urgently needed in the European theatre; that the real offensive was just starting over there; and that I was wasting my time driving an inter-island bus round the ocean, being greengrocer to the Pacific. I rashly said I would forgo rank and pay my fare back to the UK, otherwise I would be doing better to resign my commission and go back to producing food on the farm for the fighting men.

On digging this letter out of the files after 23 years I blush at my brashness; and my wife, who had been married to me only six months at the time, gives me a hard look.

However within four weeks I had received my posting and on 11 November 1943 sailed for the United Kingdom only a short time before I was to have received the bar to the DFC at an investiture to be held at the Auckland Town Hall, by the Governor-General. Sir Leonard Isitt was Chief of Air Staff then, and it was he who so helpfully commended my posting back to England, knowing how I felt in this matter.

5

Return Ticket to England

I WAS PUT IN CHARGE OF 50 New Zealand sergeant pilots who were on posting to the United Kingdom, and we sailed from Auckland on a sparkling November day. Ours was an American ship, the *Santa Monica*, dry, as all the American ships were, and the dirtiest ship I'd ever seen.

Disembarking at San Francisco we spent a few days at a military camp before entraining for New York. It took a trip like this to impress upon me the vastness of the United States; we left Oakland, California, to spend five solid days and five nights travelling through at least 10 different states before reaching our destination.

We spent 10 days at Fort Slocum in New York awaiting embarkation orders and I shan't forget going along to a large hairdressing establishment to have my hair cut: one of the barbers, on seeing my uniform, spat at me. He must have been a Nazi or a sympathiser, so I told him I'd been bombing over Germany and was going back for some more, whereupon he spat at me again. When I told my sergeant pilots about this the entire group of 50 went along to him to get their hair cut. . . .

At last our orders came through, and under cover of darkness we travelled by barge for what seemed hours up the Hudson River. In Stygian darkness we stumbled on to a pier and into an enormous wharf shed, then in a lift into the depths of a gigantic liner, where we were shown to cabins and issued with meal tickets. Although I could tell it was a big ship, I hadn't any idea it was the *Queen Elizabeth* until I saw a plan and outline of the ship on a bulkhead.

I hung around London waiting for a posting, and eventually Air Ministry told me I was to take command of 75 Squadron. Like a clot, I turned it down. I would dearly have liked to take it and felt honoured at the offer, but I was itching to get into action, and afraid that my responsibilities as a CO would keep me tied to a desk.

Having already done two tours of ops I was allowed a choice of posting and I stated a preference for some low-level daylight strafing in the new Mosquito bombers, having until now always operated at night. Air Ministry were dubious: they didn't think I was "quite the type", but I thought I was.

I had leave until early January, and most of this I spent in London, with the exception of a visit to 75 Squadron where I got mixed up in a Christmas party with such redoubtable types as Arty Ashworth, DSO, DFC, of Alexandra, Johnny Gibson, DSO, DFC, of Auckland, and the late Johnny Wright, DSO, DFC and bar, of Hamilton.

After a good time and a few pints, we became very keen to book-in for a daylight trip to the Ruhr in a Lancaster, the next day. We finally achieved our object, and at this stage, what with the fog and the grog, were convinced it was a splendid idea. The next day dawned as thick as pea soup and with a steady, misty drizzle, and the trip was scrubbed, to our great relief.

Back in London I kept calling at Halifax House to see if my posting had come through, and pestering to be allowed to join the Tactical Air Force in No 2 Group, for low-level daylight strafing. I met trouble again in the form of Al Deere and others of the same dangerous type and one day Johnny Gibson took me to the Gainsborough Studios to meet his brother-in-law, the late George Formby; but George only frowned on us for disturbing the girls on the set.

I was ordered to report at Benson, near Oxford, for an interview with Air Vice-Marshal Sir Basil Embry, and he also considered that I should go back to my old squadron. Embry was a legendary figure, and I do not think there was any one man who

Popeye Lucas's father and mother in
front of their home at Bendigo Station,
Cromwell. Mrs Lucas was a grand-
daughter of James Chapman Smith, a
pioneer settler who founded a 33,000-
acre estate

Right: November, 1936. After working his passage to England, Popeye
was accepted by the Royal Air Force for flying training at Sywell,
Northamptonshire

Popeye took his first flying lessons at Taieri with the Otago and Southland Aero Club. Here he is seen, (*third from right, back row*), with members
of the club in 1935

Popeye *(extreme right, front row)*, is seen with members of the original New Zealand Flight formed at Marham, Norfolk in July, 1939

An inspection of the New Zealand Squadron in 1940 by the New Zealand High Commissioner (Mr W. Jordan). Popeye is second from the right

The author with members of his aircrew who were flying on bomber missions over Germany from Feltwell in 1941

did more than he did in the air to help win the war, so I felt it an honour when he said he would take me in his own Mosquito up to Hertfordshire, on the following day, to join my squadron.

Next day, just after we were airborne and while still below tree-level doing about 270 mph, he seemed to be having trouble finding the right map. They were fanned out all about him, and he pulled out one after the other, but never the right one.

"Can I map-read for you, sir?" I ventured.

"No, I do it my bloody self."

So that was that, and I settled down to enjoy the flight and ignore such mundane matters as involuntary tree-topping. Of course we arrived at Hunsden in Hertfordshire in perfect safety, and found the whole station on parade to meet their AOC. The Station Commander, OC Wings and OC Squadron, were all poised at attention waiting to salute, but there was no way for the AOC to leave the aircraft until I had removed myself, which I did, trying to ignore the stony looks which greeted this anticlimax.

An old friend from my days in 3 Group was Officer Commanding Wing. This was Group Captain P. C. Pickard, famous in the F for Freddy film called *Target for Tonight* made in 1941, about Wellington bombers; he was soon to lose his life in the raid on the Amiens prison. The prison break was being planned at the time of my arrival, and as I was new to the squadron I didn't get a chance to take part. I was impressed at the efficiency and the detailed planning that went into this carefully organised raid, and the intensive use of perfectly scaled models used in this as in other raids such as that on the Mohne and Eder Dams. Precise timing was essential, and the attempt had to be made on the designated day, regardless of other factors, as on the following morning all the imprisoned French *maquis* resistance prisoners were to be shot.

Three squadrons had been chosen to take part, one British, one Australian, and one New Zealand. If the first two squadrons were unsuccessful in their mission, the third was to go in and blow the prison up, as the reprisals on the prisoners if the sortie

D

was unsuccessful were too terrible to contemplate. Lots were drawn, and the New Zealand squadron drew first on the target, to be followed by the Australians. On the morning of the raid the end of the runway was hardly visible for snow and sleet. The New Zealand squadron took off in this, and flew over the south coast, setting course for Amiens some 40 to 50 miles inland from the French coast. The first squadron successfully breached the walls, making vast gaps through which large numbers of prisoners escaped. Some prisoners and a few German guards were killed, but the raid was a success, except for the untimely loss of Group Captain Pickard who, as leader of the Wing, was shot down by a Messerschmitt while circling the target, assessing the damage done and trying to count the number of prisoners escaping.

My navigator was a chap called Tightskin – P. E. Barnes, who'd had much experience in navigating Blenheims. I never knew his given name, but Tightskin was one of the best, and determined to teach me all he knew about low-level strafing. Soon I was experiencing the thrill of below-hedge-level flying, and feeling complacent until my navigator would hit me over the head with a rolled-up map, indicating that I was to fly even lower, although I was already convinced that I was clipping the daisies. He was used to these daylight raids, flying at zero level all the way down the Rhine, and soon bullied me into his ways.

The Mosquito was a revolutionary aircraft, and the type I was flying was designated as a Mk VI fighter-bomber, powered by two 1,635-hp motors. It was made of three-ply and balsa wood, very light, strong and manoeuvrable, with four 20-mm cannon and four ·303 machine guns for armament. It was designed for low-level strafing, and carried a bomb-load of 2,000 lb which comprised two 500-lb bombs on wing-racks and two in the belly.

There were as many types of Mosquito as there were Heinz varieties. The Mark IV was a bomber and carried no armament, relying almost exclusively on speed. At this stage of the war a four-engined Flying Fortress with a crew of 11, and carrying up to 4,000 lb of bombs, took over 11 hours on the return trip to Berlin, whereas the Mark IV Mosquito bomber, with the same bomb-load, carrying no armament, and with only two as crew, could leave at dusk and complete the same trip in four hours. It was no wonder that pilots were keen to be posted to the Mosquito squadrons.

We carried out both low-level and high-level raids, as well as night-intruder ones. The aircraft was designed for a low-level cruising speed of 260 mph and when bombing at low levels, with an 11-second delay, we had to watch for the occasional bomb that bounced. The tail fin would fly off and waffle along, as also the bomb itself.

Flying so fast at ground-level made the sensation of speed even greater, and birds were as much of a menace as enemy flak. The usual tactic in our routine low-level raids was to fly across the Channel and, five minutes before ETA at the French coast, to open up to full throttle but keep down for the next minute to increase speed, then pull up to 4,000 ft, and dive across the coastline fullbore, to get below the trees as soon as possible, thus tricking the enemy radar.

As well as the night-intruder raids, on which we attacked enemy aerodromes, we made daylight attacks on flying-bomb sites, called "no-ball" targets, the code name for this type of mission. The sites were heavily camouflaged and very difficult to identify, only the peculiar ski-shaped building among the conventional farm buildings giving the lie to the pretence that this was only one more innocent farmhouse. Once pinpointed, the telltale launching pad was a final confirmation, and competition was keen among the squadrons to see who could get the most flying-bomb sites.

By this time the threat of the flying-bombs was serious, and all means were being sought to combat them. Some of the pilots in the Typhoons and Tempests used to fly alongside a flying-bomb and dip their wing under the bomb's, upsetting its gyro and causing it to spin-in before it could reach the built-up areas.

Some of the anti-aircraft batteries on the south coast of England had a hazardous job in shooting them down, as often they would land on or near a battery. These men and women showed great skill and sacrifice in preventing so many of these weapons reaching the heavily populated cities and towns.

We were shifted to Gravesend where I saw my first flying-bomb – in fact it was said to be the first to reach England. Nobody knew what it was. The sirens were wailing, and the Bofors guns going off all around the airfield. We rushed out of our tents and saw what we thought was an aircraft on fire circling the aerodrome and eventually crashing into the trees somewhere near the village of Cobham.

We were feeling sorry for the crew being incinerated in the blazing aircraft, enemy or not, but found later that it was what was to become known as a flying-bomb, doodle-bug, or VI, the blazing fuselage being in reality the tongue of flame issuing from the jet. Back in our tent one of the beds had been perforated by a huge piece of shrapnel, a jagged hole having been torn through the bedding and the camp stretcher – so it was just as well we had got up to rubberneck.

We hammered away at locating and eliminating these sites, and in the meantime it was getting near D-Day.

On my 64th op I had one engine shot out while attacking the railway yards at Charleroi in Belgium at about 50 ft. I managed to climb on one motor to 10,000 ft, but found that our fighter escort had left for home, so dived over the Channel at 350 mph to try to dodge the Messerschmitts who were always hanging around on the lookout for cripples such as ourselves.

Although the invasion was a strictly guarded secret we knew that something was brewing, and everybody was hoping for some decisive action. Although we didn't know it at the time, some 2,000 special trains had run from the north of England down to the south coast without upsetting the routine of the scheduled ones, and this gave some idea of the tremendous organisation and secrecy that had gone into the undertaking.

On 5 June I was returning from patrolling roads behind the

invasion beach-heads, and just before midnight found myself with a grandstand view of the start of D-Day. It was an eerie experience to suddenly see rows of lights, and to realise that these were aircraft towing gliders, coming in with the lights on in their aircraft, while we had been snooping behind the enemy lines in strict blackout, armed to the teeth, and expecting to be jumped by an enemy fighter at every turn.

Hundreds of gliders were going in, and the risk of collision was greater than the risk of enemy fighters, so for the first time the aircraft blackout restrictions were lifted. We were so elated at the sight, realising at once that this was the start of the great invasion, that we couldn't get back to base soon enough to refuel and be back on the job.

To our everlasting disgust we were put on reserve, and had to cool our heels and watch the Typhoons and Tempests coming in to land on our strip. The pilots would pile out of their aircraft, stretch out on their parachutes and fall immediately into exhausted sleep, while their aircraft were being re-armed and refuelled; then after that quick cat-nap they'd climb aboard and be off again.

Soon however we were put on to night patrols, patrolling a certain sector continuously, each aircraft doing an hour's patrol and then handing over to a relief. In this way there was complete coverage of all the sectors behind the invasion beach-heads, and we were gratified when our Intelligence reported that the Germans were complaining bitterly that it was bad enough to be pinned down in daylight without being hampered by the continuing need to evade marauding enemy planes by night. We felt that even if we were being denied the more spectacular jobs, at least we were making our presence felt somewhere.

I finished my 81st operation on 11 July and on 10 October found myself being flown in a Liberator from Prestwick in Scotland via Goose Bay to Montreal on posting to 45 Group, Transport Command, and I spent the next four weeks ferrying Lancasters from Canada back to Prestwick.

For a day or two I had been feeling unwell, and was uneasy that I might be sent to hospital in Montreal. If I was going to be ill I wanted to be on home ground, so organised myself to ferry back a Lancaster to Prestwick. As soon as I got in I took the night train to London, and reported to the New Zealand medical officer next day; he diagnosed pleurisy and sent me to the Royal Masonic Hospital. After nearly three weeks there I was discharged, but arrived before the Medical Board shivering and perspiring, and was immediately packed off to RAF Hospital, Halton, to be tested for tropical diseases. Exhaustive tests were made and it turned out that I had picked up some tropical bug during a one-night stopover at Guadalcanal, and so I was packed off again to hospital. On my discharge the Air Force in its wisdom posted me back to New Zealand.

I sailed in the *Rangitiki*, and was put in charge of a draft returning to New Zealand. This consisted of a hundred or so service personnel, some of their wives and fiancées, and womenfolk married or engaged to RAF personnel in New Zealand. The fair sex were a fairly mixed bunch, and I would have exchanged the task of looking after them and keeping the peace between them, any day, for a good tough bunch of sergeant pilots.

Each day brought a fresh batch of grizzles about the cramped quarters, the food, somebody else's children, etc. There were daily deputations wanting to know why they couldn't hang the baby napkins on deck as "they're going all yellow in the hold", and every morning I had to explain again why the ship was painted grey and why a line of white baby naps hanging topsides was not quite the sort of advertising we wanted with marauding submarines lying in wait for such as us.

We arrived in New Zealand in March 1945, and after the usual leave I was sent to Auckland as Station Commander at Mechanics Bay, where Combined Headquarters was established; I was there when the Japanese capitulated.

A few days after VJ-Day I looked up from my desk and saw a couple of men standing there; I guessed who they were. Considerable discontent had been generating around the Air Force stations all over the country because some civilians had been prowling around the camps with passes signed by the Minister of Defence. The general belief was that these fellows were checking on how people were doing their work, with a view to declaring them redundant.

I was disgusted when I found that these two, without making themselves known to the Station Commander, had just walked in and had been interviewing service men and women and taking down statements. They had been to the telephone operator and even to my own typist and adjutant, asking them what time I came on duty in the morning and how many days off the NCOs had, and so on.

So, when I saw them standing there full of their own importance I saw red. "Are you the Gestapo?" I asked.

There was a small silence. "I suppose we could be," replied one.

"There's no suppose about it, you are! We've had six years of war to get rid of this sort of thing. We lose all our friends and cobbers, and come home to find it on our own front doorstep."

I went straight to my desk and phoned Air Department and told the Air Commodore how strongly I felt about this. If this was to be the pattern of post-war service I was better out of it. So by 5 p.m. that afternoon I was out. Possibly the fastest ever bit of demobilisation with an honourable discharge.

For a long while my wife had been waiting to get a house or flat to live in. Accommodation was practically unprocurable, especially with two small children, and she had been lucky to have a home with her parents or mine for all the time I'd been in the United Kingdom. Now she was really looking forward to moving into the roomy flat we were taking over from Commodore Dowding, the Senior Naval Officer in New Zealand, who was being posted back to England. His wife and mine had jacked up an arrangement whereby the Dowdings were to move into an hotel, and we were to take over their flat, moving in the next day.

When I got home that night she could hardly wait to show me

some of the furnishings she had bought ready for our new home; I had to tell her that the flat was already let to someone else, that I was now a civilian, and that we were booked to travel south the next day.

So it was back to the tussocks. . . .

My official discharge came through a few days later, and after spending a couple of weeks with my parents at Moor Farm we moved into our own place at Pukepito, eight miles up the river from Balclutha, in South Otago. This 500-acre farm, which I had called Waitemata, had been grazed by my father during the war, and with no one living there except ploughmen at odd times, the homestead and buildings had become very neglected. He had bought the property, hoping I would give up flying and settle down on it. Later he helped my brothers into places of their own, leaving one to take over Moor Farm, and selling up Cranleigh, which was later cut up into four farms for soldier settlement.

It took some time to make the Waitemata farmhouse habitable. Tradesmen and building materials were hard to get, floor coverings were limited to a certain yardage, and ration coupons were still required for most necessities, especially blankets and linen. It was a big change from the gregariousness of service life, and I found it hard to settle. There was so much to be done, and not much capital to work with; it was hard to know where to start first.

After a year I began to think about flying again. The South Otago Aero Club was in the process of being revived and the thought of some flying at weekends appealed to me. I was beginning to realise that I wasn't yet ready to settle down to farming completely. I was convinced that air charter and freight work had a future.

These were already urgently needed, and communications and freight delays were bad between the North and South Islands. My experience flying the Dakota in the Pacific, and an observance of the growing demand since the end of the war, had convinced me that there was plenty of scope for civil flying. I felt that people, even the Government, had not fully realised this. It was evident that the economy was severely strained by the lack of adequate and fast freight transport throughout the whole length and breadth of New Zealand, and this was particularly acute with the bottleneck across the Cook Strait.

Our own experience of waiting *six months* for our household goods to reach us from Auckland was indication enough; even when the stuff did arrive much of it was broken and otherwise knocked about. North–south transport was completely chaotic and businessmen never ceased complaining.

It was about this time that I began to think seriously about going back into aviation commercially, and the appearance on the aviation scene of a most unusual post-war aircraft, the Bristol Freighter, opened up all sorts of possibilities.

The next few weeks saw a growing correspondence between the Bristol Aircraft Company and myself.

6

Getting off the Ground

THE FREIGHTER WAS of revolutionary design, with folding doors in the nose giving easy access for loading bulky freight into a deep and roomy fuselage. To emphasise this during demonstration trials a loaded 3-ton truck was driven into the body of the machine and flown 800 miles to its destination where, on landing, the vehicle was driven out still loaded to continue on its journey. In 1945 the Bristol was an unusual and intriguing departure from conventional aircraft design and it seemed ideal for New Zealand conditions, particularly for small fields in outback areas.

Already I had been exploring the possibility of getting a charter and freight service operating from Bluff or Invercargill to the North. Numerous men whose businesses depended on the quick transport of their goods were most enthusiastic, and their support and offers of finance were assured. A papermill gave a promise of a 5-ton payload to Auckland six days a week.

My solicitors and I personally had written to the Minister of Civil Aviation and to the Prime Minister, but the results were not promising. The replies stated quite baldly that permission would not be granted, because all internal air services were to be reserved for the National airline. In the meantime an application to the Controller of Customs brought a reply, that although a licence would be granted to import the plane specified, it was very unlikely that permission would be given to operate it after entry into the country.

However once I knew that the aircraft could be imported, I filed one application after another in the hope that some satisfaction could be gained. Interviews with National Airways Corporation officers only reaffirmed that the Government (not the officers themselves) were stubbornly against private enterprise in this field, and that it was hopeless to attempt to get permission from the authorities.

The next application, however, brought the concession that the licence *might* be granted, but only on the condition that the routes to be allocated through NAC would not conflict with their existing ones. I was overjoyed, thinking that now we were getting somewhere; but the application to NAC dashed all hopes. They replied advising that there were no routes left to operate!

It was now early 1946, and commercial aviation in New Zealand was only in its infancy, as was the National Airways Corporation itself. It was obvious that it would be several years before the Corporation would be in a position to operate any of the feeder services that were being sought by just a few of us now, but later by an ever-increasing number of ex-service pilots intent on establishing themselves in a post-war world.

Then the Bristol Aircraft Company, who were anxious to start selling their new aeroplane, wrote to say that they were bringing out a Freighter to New Zealand on a publicity tour, and I was invited to be present as a potential buyer.

I had now spent 18 months of time-consuming and costly petitioning to be allowed to bring this aeroplane in, and to use it opening up the back country and freighting between the North and South Islands. I had got precisely nowhere, and so it was especially disappointing to know that the Freighter was coming to New Zealand and that I could make no plans to go ahead with its use.

The publicity over my attempts to obtain a licence for a Bristol Freighter had come to the attention of Bill Hewett of Gore. Early in July 1947 he called on me to explore the possibility of my joining him in the operation of a small charter service at Queenstown. I had just taken delivery of an Auster Autocrat, a single-engined, three-seater, high-winged mono-plane, the second of its type to be imported into New Zealand.

This could be used to form the nucleus of an aerial venture, and so Bill's idea appealed to me.

We trudged over all the 500 acres of the farm, deliberating. We inspected stock and fences, about which Bill knew nothing and cared less, chewing over the possibilities of this idea. Finally after he'd seen every item of interest, cattle, sheep, woolshed, turnip paddock, I took him back to the farmhouse for a much-needed drink. Then over afternoon tea, before a roaring winter's fire, I told him I would join him. He was of course pleased, but thoroughly disgusted when I told him later that I had already made up my mind before taking him on the marathon around the farm.

"I thought I'd make you sweat awhile," I said.

But Bill was making me sweat before many weeks were past. In our early discussions he'd told me he had a Proctor I which he'd operated the year before on scenic and charter flights at Queenstown, in company with his friend Tex Smith of Gore, who had since returned to the building trade. With this aeroplane and my new Auster, we intended to form a partnership and get started as soon as possible, as the West Coast whitebait season opened in September and the Queenstown tourist season in December. Bill had omitted however to tell me that his Proctor was unserviceable. It was even then being transported in pieces to Christchurch for repair. A mishap at the Frankton Aerodrome, in which he had his first experience of what ice on the wings can do to the aerodynamics of an aeroplane, had caused him to try conclusions with a fence. Of course he expected to have the aeroplane serviceable again before the partnership was finalised.

Now I went ahead with plans to sell the farm and move to Queenstown. The Land Sales Department was operating then, and looking back over old correspondence I wonder why I bothered to find a buyer. At the price set I might as well have given it away. It was quickly sold, and by the end of August we were ready to leave.

At Queenstown board or rented accommodation was almost

non-existent. Most houses available were holiday homes, let only for short periods at a time. We were at last able to buy a small cottage, once the stationmaster's residence when the New Zealand Railway wharf was situated half-way out to Frankton, at the bottom of Battery Hill. It was a nondescript little house, but in a pleasant position at the lakeside, commanding magnificent views of the mountains on all sides, and a tranquil view of the Kawarau Falls Bridge seen through weeping willows fringing the lake edge. Some old-established apricot trees, and a number of shrubs and fruit trees planted by ourselves, redeemed what would otherwise have been a rather bleak spot.

Originally Bill and I were to have been partners on an equal basis, but we needed an engineer, and Bill suggested inviting a friend of his to join us. This was done and so on 9 September 1947 the company was formed, with Bill and me as pilots and Barry Topliss of Nelson as engineer. With my family settled in at the cottage by the lake, Bill and I started to put the old buildings at the aerodrome in order for us as company premises. The place had once been the local racecourse, and the old grandstand was still there but had fallen into disrepair.

Bill had lived in the only habitable part of the building during his flying operations of the season before, and this single room and a long stone wall were all that was usable. Board and lodgings were unprocurable so my wife, Lorie, made a spare room available for Bill, and later on for other members of the firm, including the engineer and his wife and family, until they could find alternative accommodation elsewhere. This put rather a strain on our slender financial resources, on the limited capacity of our small house, and on the physical resources of Lorie, who already had plenty to do caring for our young family, tending a large garden, and answering the telephone and making bookings for the firm.

Our first official flight was made on 8 September in the Auster, freighting whitebait out from Jackson Bay and Big Bay in South Westland. On 11 September a week after Bill and I had started dismantling part of the old buildings, a section of the wall collapsed on me. With a terrific effort Bill managed to heave it off me, then raced to the hospital a few hundred yards away to get help, while I lay in choking dust, with an excruciating pain in the hip. I was carried on a stretcher to the Frankton Hospital theatre, where our local doctor, Dr Bill Anderson, author of *Doctor in the Mountains*, re-set my dislocated hip. He did a fine job, and I can be grateful to him that I received no permanent disability. It taxed all his strength to get it back into place, he told me later, as he had no proper facilities at the hospital for such a manipulation. On the following day, Bill Hewett was interested to note that he couldn't even lift the wall he had tossed aside so frantically the evening before.

The accident couldn't have come at a worse time. We were anxious to get some shelter and to start building a hangar. The whitebait season had already started, and the scenic and charter work was beginning to build up. By this time the engineer had moved his family down from Christchurch, and we had Trevor Cheetham, also of Christchurch, as our first employee. He had been an instructor with the RNZAF in the latter stages of the war, and had about 500 hours up when he came to us. He was a fine pilot, and a loyal and hardworking member of the firm, by whom he is still employed, although he has given up flying and now works in an administrative capacity. In the early days he divided his time between flying duties and the office. Later he was given shares and made a director in recognition of his services, but relinquished these at a later date for personal reasons.

It was always a sore point with Bill that he had been unable to get overseas; he had an arm disability which prevented him from serving outside New Zealand. He'd badgered the authorities until at last he got himself accepted for aircrew in the RNZAF. But having got this far, the war packed up! If he had gone overseas, there is no doubt that he would have made a name for himself – if he had lived long enough. He was of the stuff and temperament to make a fighter ace: a natural pilot with a reserve of dash and devilry and rash courage. It wasn't to be, however, and this streak of rashness on many occasions in later years got him off-side with the powers-that-be, while his extraordinary ability as a pilot has brought him safely through numerous incidents and escapades.

While I was still in hospital Bill and Trevor were carrying on with the flying and getting the premises in some sort of order. There was only my Auster ZK-APO to fly as Bill's Proctor was still at Christchurch on repair and overhaul, and whitebaiting on the coast was in full swing.

7

Prospects: Uncertain

B IG BAY, also known as Awarua Bay, is a fascinating area. Isolated, in South Westland, 50 miles as the crow flies from Queenstown, it looks out across the Tasman Sea. Jackson Bay is 60 miles up-coast to the north, and Martins Bay and Milford Sound to the south. Big Bay is a hard strip of sand bounded by heavy bush and forest and the beach is perfect to land on – at low tide. Farther up, soft sand creates a hazard, and buried driftwood can cause trouble. The Skippers and Red Hill Ranges lie to the east, and sandhills form a natural barrier to the incoming tide. Although only 40 minutes by air from Queenstown, it is a rugged three or more days' journey in on foot.

Our usual flight route was up Lake Wakatipu to Glenorchy, through the Rockburn along the Olivine to Lakes Alabaster and Wilmot, up the Pyke River, and into Big Bay at the top of Skippers Range. Alternatively, when the weather was poor, we flew up the Greenstone Valley, down the Hollyford River, and out on to the West Coast, or sometimes up Lake Wanaka, through the Haast Pass, and down the coast past Jackson Bay.

The one and only regular resident in this big, wild, empty area at that time was the late Davy Gunn of Deadman's Bluff in the Hollyford Valley. He regularly travelled into and about the Big Bay country, escorting parties of tourists or rounding up his cattle, which he grazed there under lease. He had several huts, one at Big Bay and others at Martins Bay. Davy was well known and respected, and will always be remembered for his epic feat in going for help after a plane crash at Big Bay in 1936,

wartime picture
...en in Trafalgar
...uare, London. Be-
...e returning to New
...land Popeye had
...npleted two tours
...perations and won
...FC with bar

Loraine (Lorie) Flans-
burgh-Washbourne be-
came Mrs Lucas in 1943.
She was with the WAAF,
stationed at Whenuapai,
where Popeye was posted
soon after returning to New
Zealand

Four of the crew which was the first to fly No. 40 Transport Squadron's first Dakota in New Zealand: *(left to right)* Sgt Fred Meyer, F.O. Douglas Newall, DFC, Popeye, and Sgt E. Robson. Missing from the photograph is Flying Officer Lloyd Parry, the second pilot

The first Dakota at Whenuapai was appropriately emblazoned with the insignia of its Captain

in which one person was killed and three others and the pilot injured.

The rainfall is about 200 in. annually and it seems to be at its greatest during the whitebait season, which is from 1 September until the end of November. Flying over this country is awe-inspiring. Below is a continuing panorama of purple-shadowed abysses; there are jagged, upsurging peaks, fog-enshrouded or snow-capped, and mile upon mile of pinnacles, ravines, and icefields. It is a place of immense silences, broken only by the noise of your own engines and by the roar of falling avalanches in the spring. We flew in vast blue spaces, or into lowering storm clouds, always watching the green rain-forest below for open riverflats, or clearings suitable for forced landings. I never had to make one here, but it became second nature to locate and remember all such places for possible future reference.

During this first season we were plagued by bad weather and lack of communications, culminating in the near-destruction of the Auster, when it was forced down on the Lammerlaw Range, a rough and inhospitable place about 45 miles from Dunedin. The aeroplane was caught in a down-draught and Bill had to crash-land with a full load of whitebait into a snow-filled, inaccessible gully. He was uninjured, and fortunately knew the country well enough to make his way 12 miles to the nearest habitation. It was three weeks before we could get the Auster dismantled and sledged out in sections, and it practically had to be rebuilt in Christchurch.

This was really serious. The whitebait were running fast, and the whitebaiters at Big Bay were depending on regular planes to bring in food and stores and freight out the highly perishable catch. There was much heartburning over the 450 lb of whitebait lost in the Lammerlaw crash. At this time the fishermen had not installed the holding nets which later were found to be so valuable, and many pounds of bait had to be dumped during that season owing to poor flying conditions and no radio communication.

Without a serviceable aeroplane we were out of business

E

before we had got fairly started, but my father stepped into the breach and lent us money for another aeroplane, although he had no great love for aeroplanes or faith in the aviation industry. He'd have preferred to see me back on the land. So within a few days we had added Proctor Mark I ZK-APG to the company register. It wasn't the machine we wanted, but at the time very few suitable aeroplanes were available.

Then on 29 October 1947, exactly one month later, Bill, flying the new Proctor, became overdue on a whitebait flight from Big Bay. It wasn't until late on the following day that an RNZAF Hudson from Wigram on Search and Rescue duty located it, nose embedded in the soft sand, at Big Bay. Bill was unhurt but he'd spent a grim three hours hanging on to the machine, up to his chest in water, as the rising tide and pounding surf threatened to break it in pieces in the undertow. Finally with the help of the whitebaiters he managed to secure it safely above high tide mark. Although comparatively little damage had been done initially, it was a costly salvage. Harry Wigley of the Mount Cook and Southern Lakes Tourist Company, who had taken part in the search for the overdue aircraft, flew in the engineer, Barry Topliss, to make an inspection, and brought Bill out.

Spares were needed for the stranded Proctor but now no other aircraft owner would risk his plane over there, or even bring one through to Queenstown. It had become purgatory for me to stay lying in hospital waiting for news of more overdue aeroplanes, so I discharged myself and went home. Having fruitlessly tried to persuade one of the aero clubs to bring spares through by air, I decided to take my car and drive through to Timaru myself to collect the spares so urgently needed. Trevor came with me for company as I still felt a little shaky.

We set out on the nightlong drive, expecting to be home in the early hours of the morning, but on our way home Trevor rolled the car. In thick fog he had mistaken a loading ramp at the side of the road for a turn-off. The car rolled over into a field, and half the spares were thrown out and lost in the long grass stiff with frost. It was 3.30 a.m., but we were able to rouse a garageman who pulled us out. It was bitterly cold searching by torchlight, trying to find the scattered spare parts. Some we never found.

We drove on back to Queenstown, arriving in time for breakfast, and in time to assuage the anxieties of my wife and mother-in-law who were becoming more and more concerned about our non-appearance. The car was badly damaged, with crumpled bodywork and some broken windows, Trevor was limping from a bruised leg, and I had a gash on my head that looked worse than it was. Lorie's face was a study when we walked in through the door.

Our race against time had been wasted as the next few days were out for flying anyway; the weather was shocking. However when it cleared we were able to persuade the South Canterbury Aero Club to fly the spares and stores into Big Bay. The Tiger Moth therefore was flown into Queenstown on 4 November, but in view of his greater knowledge of the area and still poor weather, Trevor Cheetham took over from the club pilot on arrival, and flew into Big Bay. Soon after he left the weather began to clamp down again very quickly, and before long Trevor had become overdue. By now the weather was so bad that no search aircraft could consider trying to locate him, and though we were fairly sure that he was marooned at Big Bay nobody could take it for granted.

As soon as it was possible, search aircraft went in and found him on the beach, crash-landed and with no hope of flying out until substantial repairs had been made. He'd had an uneventful trip in, and offloaded his spares and supplies, but by the time he was heading for home the weather had started closing in very quickly. He had pressed on, hoping to get over the saddle on to the Queenstown side of the Alps before the cloud came too far down, but had to turn back to Big Bay. Fuel was getting low, and the incoming tide had already covered the firm safe part of the beach, and he'd had no alternative but to chance a landing on the treacherous soft sand higher up. He might just have made it, but an extra big wave caught the Tiger on touch-down and neatly flipped it on its back. Trevor was unhurt, but the aeroplane had been badly damaged by the heavy surf.

These incidents highlighted the very real need for proper radio communications in this type of country. The West Coast weather was notoriously tricky and could change very rapidly. Ever since we had started flying into Big Bay we had been begging the Post and Telegraph Department for permission to operate our own commercial radio, but so far had been refused, though we had the equipment already set up and waiting at the aerodrome.

One might have hoped that this mishap would mark the end of our run of bad luck; but three days later, while Lorie was ironing, the primus she was using to heat up the flat-iron blew up, and the exploding fuel set the kitchen walls alight. She rushed to smother the flaming curtains that had fallen down over our four-year-old son Richard and set his hair and pyjamas on fire. Her mother, who was staying with us at the time, with great presence of mind beat out the flames with mats off the floor and basins of water. At the expense of some painful burns to her arms she saved the house, which was tinder-dry, and would have been an inferno in a few minutes. I had been to evening service at St Peter's Anglican Church at Queenstown, and the excitement was all over by the time I got home.

More was to come. We put the routine report into the insurance company for repairs to the car, which would be quite extensive, only to be informed that the policy was void. I had stated in the accident report that Trevor had been the driver, but I hadn't known that he hadn't renewed his driving licence. This was a great blow, coming on top of all the other incidents and expenses. Fortunately after some correspondence the insurance company agreed to honour the claim. Lorie drove the car over to Cromwell to be railed to Dunedin for repairs, and perhaps our luck was in after all, for when she pulled up at the railway yards another car roared to a standstill beside hers. The driver, greatly perturbed, had been desperately trying to stop her for the last few miles through the Kawarau Gorge. He wanted to tell her that the rear wheel was almost off. As they examined it, the last nut fell off the last thread. At the speed she had been travelling through the Gorge she would have finished up 100 ft down into the river if the wheel had parted company on that stretch of the road.

After this things settled down a little, and our son David was born six weeks late, despite all the alarums and excursions, and much to the disgust of my wife who found Christmas disrupted, and had to spend New Year in the nursing home. My mother-in-law, who had come down to help and look after the family, had long overstayed her time to be away, and had to leave before the new grandson was brought home, much to her disappointment and ours.

The Proctor was repaired and flown out, and the Tiger Moth, although written-off by the insurance company, was salvaged by Mish Toole and Wattie Wilmot and flown out to Timaru.

Once we had stopped making unpleasant headlines, we settled down to erecting the hangar and doing the daily scenic flights which were now building up. At this period demobilised servicemen were still taking advantage of their travel concessions, and steady numbers of our fellow-countrymen were having their first glimpse of the South Island and the scenic wonders of Fiordland. Many of them were combining their trip with a honeymoon.

We were busy building the hangar out of blue-gum poles, cut and dragged to the site with the help of my 1936 Plymouth. This building material was dictated not only by the lack of finance but by the shortage of materials after the end of the war. Everything was still rationed, obtainable only on receipt of the necessary permits. It took weeks to get these approved and, apparently just as a matter of principle, any amount requested was automatically cut by half. One day we went away up the Skippers Canyon to salvage an abandoned steel hawser from an old mining site, for use in the erection of the hangar. We wanted

to do our own maintenance overhauls, but couldn't get permission to do so until we had built the hangar and workshop in
compliance with the requirements of the Civil Aviation Department.

We were handicapped too by a lack of finance; Bill's capital
was the value of his aircraft, as was mine, and Barry had only
$100 paid up of his shares, so we were desperately in need of
working capital. My father had loaned money for the purchase
of the Proctor I, for some time at no interest, and later at a very
nominal rate. This lack of finance was always to be a crippling
factor. We were chronically under-capitalised. We couldn't
qualify for a Returned Serviceman's Loan, as so many others
were doing, to get established: when we applied the Department
ruled that the aviation business was "too risky".

It had been our intention to do our own Certificate of Airworthiness overhauls to save maintenance costs, but we found
that Barry did not have the necessary qualifications, so we did
not actually do our own C of As until 1955 when Eric Ewington,
an English wartime friend of Barry's, joined the firm, and has
proved indispensable ever since.

Finally, with the hangar almost finished, we made a trip to
the abandoned mining town of Macetown in the Arrowtown
district, to collect some roofing iron for the hangar. Iron, like
everything else, was practically unprocurable, and in any case
rationed. Although this was difficult to recover it was worth-
while as now we had shelter, with hangar space and a small
workshop.

These months were marked by a continuation of the paper
war with Air Department and National Airways. I had by now
shelved the idea of the Bristol Freighter service between Invercargill and Auckland, and settled down to getting on with our
present venture. Our applications became involved in an unend-
ing shuttle back and forth between Air Department and
NAC. Although with little hope now of achieving our objective
we stepped up the correspondence from a monthly to a weekly
basis. At least the replies came sooner.

From the day we had formed the company we had petitioned the Government to allow us to operate air charter, air taxi and air freight services, and to let us provide feeder services to NAC's main trunk lines. We applied to have airfields licensed at many different places, including Glenorchy and Wanaka. We wanted to get the Cromwell airfield re-licensed, and we wanted to operate feeder services into these areas, and mercy services into the back country when required. I was convinced that better and quicker access would open up these areas much more quickly, especially Queenstown, whose tourist potential was so apparent.

Glenorchy was 20 minutes by air from Queenstown, and already we had made a number of mercy flights. Each one was illegal, and each one had laid us open to disciplinary action from the Civil Aviation Department, but all had been necessary to save a human life. At this time too, we applied for a licence to operate an air service for passengers and freight through Central Otago, with the terminus at Frankton, and also for a direct tourist service between Queenstown and Rotorua. These of course were turned down, and had we known that it would be July 1950 before we would be allowed to establish our air service for Central Otago, I doubt if we'd have had the heart to persevere.

By January 1948 we had progressed as far as a meeting of local bodies, and matters of policy concerning air services were discussed. Our Government at this time was a Labour one, as was that of the United Kingdom, and was pledged to the policy of national socialism, but while ours was firmly against private enterprise entering the field of aviation, the British Government was encouraging extensive charter flying.

Two opposition members, Mr J. Roy, member for Clutha, and Mr T. L. (now Sir Thomas) MacDonald, made efforts in the House to impress the Government with the urgent need for air communications between Dunedin and the country district. I felt that NAC needed a network of feeder services to provide a steady flow of passengers and freight to their main services, and that it could be best supplied by private operators. If we had to wait for NAC to serve these areas their progress and development would be set back decades. But in Parliament, when the Aviation Bill was being considered, the Minister of Finance made it clear that he would not license private operators to run air taxi or charter services, as in later years the Government would have to buy them out at a huge price. This may have been a reasonable assumption on the Government's part, but we wanted to get going, and we wanted to open up-country, and we wanted progress, and the Government could look after their own headaches.

Central Otago at this time was the most poorly served district for aviation in the whole of New Zealand, though farther north there was quite a network of air services even over many well road-serviced areas. I always felt that we were in an area full of potential, and one which could be richly productive, but we were shut off from progress not only by semi-isolation, poor roads and mountain ranges, but by pigheaded officialdom. No province was more in need of air services to open it up.

Altogether, 1947 was a disappointing year, beset with every kind of bad luck, difficulty, and frustration. Still, the future seemed pretty bright: the need of air services in the area was beyond dispute, material shortages *must* lessen as the months went by, and all our company needed was a break of just average luck. Our enthusiasm, experience and endurance would do the rest.

8

Fish, Deer, Rabbits

THE NEW YEAR started off quite well. We had already passed the turnover figure we needed to keep in business, and provided we had no more prangs the future looked pretty bright. Any work was good work. During the season we flew fresh-gathered tomatoes to Gore, Balclutha, Invercargill, and Dunedin. The growers would pick them the night before, and we would have them at the markets by 8 a.m. next day. We did sheep-spotting for farmers on near-by runs, and at the Branches Station beyond Mt Aurum at the head of Skippers Canyon the owners had us spot for a cattle muster. Accompanying me in the plane, they counted the cattle and marked their positions on a map, together with notes and instructions. After we had thoroughly checked the area, I flew low and dropped the map and instructions to the men waiting below at the musterers' camp.

Queenstown was always short of fresh fish, and for a while we were in business as flying fishmongers. We brought back fresh fish from Timaru as a backload after freighting whitebait to the main city centres. There was a distribution problem on arrival at Queenstown, and so the quickest way for us to dispose of the fish fresh was by hawking it ourselves. We'd load it into my car or the old aerodrome truck, a 1929 Chrysler, and drive to Queenstown or Arrowtown. Sea fish, being scarce, was always much sought after, and once the word got round we were surrounded by a crowd and the whole load was soon gone.

Work increased so rapidly that by next season we didn't bother to go on with this; it took time and was too tiring. Quite often we had been up at 3 or 4 a.m. to fly into Big Bay to catch an early tide and uplift the whitebait. If there was a big catch there would be freighting trips not only to Dunedin and Invercargill but to Christchurch as well, as we didn't want to glut the markets. Often there'd be a return trip in on the afternoon tide. After a long day like this none of us felt much like hawking fish around the countryside. Usually Trevor and I, or Bill and I, and sometimes the three of us went on these hawking trips. After the initial drudgery we always felt virtuous about our visits to the local hostelries at Arrowtown, or calling in at the Lower Shotover Hotel to see Vic Gerkin on the way back to Frankton.

Farmers were quick to see the advantages and speed of air freight, and we had numerous requests for urgent delivery of spare parts needed to repair machinery that had broken down in the middle of haymaking or shearing. Occasionally after making whitebait deliveries to Invercargill we backloaded Bluff oysters to Dunedin on transfer to the National Airways Lodestars and Dakotas, for urgent freight to the northern centres.

In February 1948 Miss Ruth Adams of Christchurch fell during an ascent on Mt La Perouse, and a full-scale rescue operation went into action. Organisations were alerted to help, and we offered our services in any capacity, as did many others, including the gallant ground parties and the guides who made the rescue possible. Bill Hewett picked up Miss Adams's father and Mr Alec Graham from the airfield of Franz Josef Glacier, and they circled the rescue party at the foot of La Perouse, dropping supplies of food by parachute, and a note of encouragement from father to daughter.

At this time I was trying to interest the Wild Life section of Internal Affairs in using aircraft in their deer-culling activities. RNZAF Dakotas were being used to drop supplies to the cullers in various places, but the Dakota was limited however to dropping on a restricted number of sites, one of them being a strip we were already using in the Alps at the lower end of the Landsborough River. I even had to land on one or two occasions to check up for the Department on the accuracy of the drops being made by the Dakota. To me this seemed a waste of manpower and machines: the deer-cullers had still to pack the stores-drop miles back into their top huts, using up a lot of valuable shooting-time on non-productive work. My idea of efficient supply-dropping was to be the flying grocer and drop the stuff right at the hut door.

On 7 February 1948 I was making experimental parachute drops on the Frankton aerodrome, trying to find the best way of packing supplies, the best types of 'chutes to use, and to see what happened in "free" drops. I did one of the first actual drops on 14 February at Monowai, and shortly after did another one up the Clarence River near Kaikoura. Ron Fraser, of the Wild Life section, did recces with me around the Molesworth area and the Kaikouras. I took other Internal Affairs officers to spot for sites for deer-cullers' camps and flew the cullers into the Landsborough. Then I dropped hut materials into the Upper Clarence. It wasn't much to start with, but the work built up very quickly, especially after the Ministry of Works lost their Proctor in a fatal crash at Monowai.

Most of our work was done through Ron Fraser, a very able officer. Right from the start he could see the potential of aircraft. I have worked with other officers over the years, and have had the happiest associations with them.

Supply-dropping was to become one of our most important jobs, providing a good steady income and helping us to fully utilise our aircraft. We used to supply-drop for the Department almost exlusively, but in later years shared some of the work with the helicopter operators.

The Forest Service, which took over Wild Life in 1956 – later it became its Noxious Animals division – wasted no time in devising the best ways to drop their supplies. The bulk of their stuff was flour, yeast, tinned and dehydrated foods, and ammunition. Experience soon taught them which stores were best dropped by parachute, and which would survive a free drop. After experiment we found that the best way to pack the stores for a free drop was in one bag contained in a larger one. If the inner one burst on impact, the outer one stayed intact, and safely contained the goods. No vital stores got spread over the terrain and, if packed with forethought, nothing was spoilt by violently-opposing mixtures in the same bag. Flour and sugar, tents, and other similar goods were usually let go in a free drop, that is, without a parachute. In our earliest days the Auster could carry about 460 lb plus the thrower-out, but later when we got the De Havilland Dominies, they proved great old work-horses, carrying three times as much, and with room for the thrower-out in much more comfort.

The alpine clubs too, were not slow to make use of the new medium, and we did many drops for them over the years. Christmas and Easter were the peak times. They gave us photographs and a briefing before they started out on their climbs, usually taking enough food with them to last for several days. This was important, as on one or two early occasions the odd party had gone in completely trusting that the drop would arrive to the day and on the minute. Weather however always has the final say and quite often the weather would begin to deteriorate just as soon as the party left. Several days might elapse before it was possible to action the drop, especially in the Southern Alps, where the passes are often closed off with low cloud. It created problems for us too, knowing that a party was entirely dependent on us for food. On these occasions the sense of emergency often encouraged a pilot to make a trip, flying in risky conditions and very much against his own judgement.

We passed on the tips we had learnt from experiments in packing and dropping for the Forestry, but sometimes a group would do their own packing away from the aerodrome, or occasionally because they thought they needed no advice, and there'd be some weird results. Some of the recipients got strange mixtures of tea and jelly, squashed butter and condensed milk, concertina'd tins of fruit, and burst bags of flour and sugar mixed indiscriminately with snow, ice, or river silt.

. . . . .

Apart from the scenic and charter work and a miscellany of other jobs we sought further avenues on the aerial farming side. There seemed scope in all directions.

Rabbit-poisoning was one of these and later on was to prove, together with supply-dropping, the backbone of our aerial work. On 6 September 1948 I think we did the first aerial rabbit-poisoning in the country. The job was done for Duncan Anderson of Bog Roy Station, Omarama. Pellets of poisoned pollard were dropped over several thousand acres of hill country, and the results were so encouraging that Duncan made immediate plans for more aerial poisoning the following season. He accompanied me on the job, and at first our facilities were pretty primitive. The pollard pellets had to be mixed by hand and fed through an improvised hopper made out of an egg-pulp tin; it was hard, dirty work.

Duncan Anderson's pioneering effort paved the way for more extensive and concentrated use of poisoning from the air. The rabbit boards showed an immediate interest in the results of his experiments, and the results obtained at Bog Roy, and in August 1949 we made more experiments with the Otekaieke Board, and dropped phosphorised pollard over the islands in the Waitaki River and on Kurow Hill. That season too we laid poison at Queenstown, Glendhu Bay, Wanaka, Tarras, Cardrona, Hawea Flat, and Alexandra. Also for a number of other boards, including Omarama, and the Upper Waihao.

One of the major difficulties affecting the rabbit Boards all over the country was the lack of finance and trained manpower. Therefore the boards, the North Otago ones particularly, were quick to see the potential saving in time and labour if aerial poisoning could be proved practical. According to figures drawn up at the time it took one man one day to lay 20 lb of poison on hill country. Therefore it would take 112 men to spread one ton in one day, and the cost in wages would be about $350. In comparison the cost of aerial poisoning, depending upon distance from the airstrip, was between $30 and $40 per ton, and this ton could be spread in one hour.

The results from this, the first season's operations on a commercial basis by the boards, were very encouraging. We got a high percentrage of kills, on occasions almost 100 per cent, and the boards weren't slow to catch on. Aerial rabbit-poisoning was here to stay. It was exciting, and we had all the work we could handle. More aircraft became a necessity, and rabbit-poisoning became our major work during the winter months, just at a time when the tourist season was fairly dormant. It enabled us to use what aircraft we had to their full capacity, and gave long hours of flying to the pilots, who valued the extra hours for the bonus they received above their basic wage.

In the early days the hopper in the Auster carried only 50 lb. We were sowing pollard poison then, and it was difficult to make this flow smoothly. One man sat behind the pilot, tipping poison into the hopper from sugar-bags, of which there'd be about 14 full ones stacked all about him. It was cramped and tiring work, and he had constantly to work a hand agitator to keep the contents of the hopper running smoothly.

Eventually we put in a full-sized hopper with a wind-driven agitator. This could take about 500 lb, and the chopped-up carrot bait was tipped in manually from outside (by this time the choice of poison and bait had progressed from the original phosphorised poison pollard). Barry Topliss was constantly exercising his brains and ingenuity, thinking up the best type and design of hopper for these operations. Once we had installed the bigger hoppers capable of being loaded externally before take-off, we had no need to carry a man to check the flow and feed the hopper.

After several seasons we had four Austers spreading 30 to 40 tons of poison a day, doing nothing else for weeks on end. One winter we put out over 1,200 tons of carrots. The boards went on to use different types of poison besides other means of eradication. Phosphorus was soon discarded in favour of strychnine, and then this gave way to arsenic. Finally sodium fluoracetate, commonly known as 1080, became almost universally used. It was tasteless, odourless, and with no known antidote; a dangerous poison but much easier to handle than strychnine or arsenic.

These later methods were an improvement on the phosphorised pollard, which caused a lingering death, producing an intense thirst which drove the affected rabbits to the nearest water. This caused a problem in some parts of the MacKenzie Country where the poisoned rabbits would get carried along in the race water and become jammed in the nozzle of some private power plant providing water to a homestead.

The boards contracted with the growers for high-grade carrots to be used with the poison for feeding out to the rabbits. These were chopped into pieces and mixed with the poison in a concrete-mixer, which was set up right beside the airstrip from which the aircraft was working. Usually two feeds were given at intervals with unpoisoned carrots, or bait as it was called. The rabbits fed on this, and finding it edible and with no harmful effects were unsuspecting when the third, poisoned, bait was laid.

In most cases we got excellent kills, but on one board there was a problem. For two seasons in succession arsenic poison had been laid, but no good result had been obtained. The area had been indiscriminately shot over by deerstalkers and weekend shooters. The board thought this constant traffic had made the rabbits unsettled and nervous, and may have made them suspicious of the bait.

A plan was worked out. Just before the next poisoning operation the board arranged with the farmer to take all his stock off the place, and all shooting and other traffic in the area was barred. When the six months' waiting period was up I was engaged to lay three lots of unpoisoned feed. But just when I was ready to make the final lethal poison lay, an extremely heavy snowfall threatened to spoil the operation. Luckily I was able to complete the job despite the weather, and we got an absolutely 100 per cent kill. On inspection, there was not a living thing on the property. Even six sheep and an old horse that had wandered on to the empty block were dead, plus a couple of deer.

Different to the days when some parts of this country were almost a moving mass of rabbits, and some farm properties had in the early days been abandoned because of the rabbit pest.

The boards made every effort to work in with the farmer to prevent any poisoning of stock, but sometimes accidents happened. One of the drawbacks in the use of 1080 is that nobody knows how long it stays lethal. It is thought to last about three months, and if there has been plenty of rain, it is then fairly safe to put stock back on to the block. However some farmers have been caught with poison laid months before. This is usually when there has been a dry spell, and the poisoned carrot had dried up and become inedible. Then with the first rain it swells up and becomes edible again. It is a problem for the rabbit boards today. With properties now carrying far more stock, the farmer hasn't enough grazing to close up blocks indefinitely, and it may well be that the boards will have to go back to arsenic or similar poison.

It has been gratifying in later years to see how aerial poisoning has helped in the rabbit extermination policy. When I first came to Queenstown in 1947 the hills through the Kawarau Gorge and all the neighbouring country, in fact the whole district, seemed to move with rabbits. On a drive along a country road, there would be dozens of dead rabbits run over by cars. At night they would run into the glare of headlights from all sides, and it was almost impossible to avoid running over at least one in a short drive.

Flying down the Kawarau Gorge in those days an observer would get the impression that this was uninhabited country unable to support any life except the rabbits that one could see in thousands, running for cover at the noise of the aircraft engines. The mountain slopes were barren, denuded of vegetation and tussock. Today this same area looks like a different world; there is any amount of cover and growth, and the tussock is regenerating. It is unusual to see a rabbit at all in some places.

1944. 487 New Zealand Squadron at Hunsdon, Hertfordshire. Popeye, then flying Mosquito aircraft, is first from the right, front row

With Air Commodore M. W. Buckley at RNZAF Reception Centre, Wellington in 1945. Air Commodore Buckley had previously instructed Popeye in Wellington aircraft, been his flight commander, squadron commander, station commander and group commander, and is godfather of David, one of Popeye's sons

On 9 September, 1947, Popeye formed his commercial flying company with Bill Hewett and Barry Topliss. The first flight in the company's Auster aircraft was freighting whitebait from Jackson Bay and Big Bay in South Westland. Later a Proctor, shown in the picture at Big Bay, was also used freighting whitebait

Whitebaiters checking their nets at high tide on the Awarua River. Big Bay, also known as Awarua Bay, is a remote and fascinating area. But while it is a rugged three or four days' journey from Queenstown on foot, the trip could be completed by air in forty minutes

It has been said that complete extermination is an impossibility, and it may well be so, but I feel that the policy of complete extermination should be aimed at at all times. It has been estimated by the "boffins" that the present low level of rabbit infestation has allowed the ewe population to increase by seven millions. An unguarded increase in rabbits could see the grazing for these sheep and for seven million more disappear before our eyes.

Perhaps I've digressed too much about the rabbits? But every New Zealander with any feeling for the land in his veins regards Mr Rabbit as a deadly enemy, and I look back on the help we were able to give to Duncan Anderson in the early days, and our large-scale operations later, with particular satisfaction.

9

Mainly Topdressing

NOW WE WERE STARTING into the 1948 whitebait season still without any licences, and no proper radio contact. This we felt had to be remedied especially after the mishaps of the previous season. Those incidents at Big Bay need never have happened if we had been allowed to use our radio telephone.

During these months too, we had continued to plug away at the Air Department for a licence to carry freight. As this still wasn't forthcoming we had now to resign ourselves to another season of pirating. In order to operate without being prosecuted, we bought the whitebait direct from the fishermen at Big Bay. There was nothing illegal in carrying our own property, and we thus avoided the trap of carrying things "for hire and reward". Within this framework we were able to stay on the right side of the law.

But without radio, the whitebaiters had no way of knowing whether the aeroplane could get in. The weather over there might seem OK to them but often we couldn't get over the Pass. We'd make the attempt but would be forced to turn back time and time again, taking risks because we knew that the 'baiters would by now have all the catch packed into 40-lb tins and shouldered down to the beach, waiting for the aeroplane. After all that hard work, and knowing the price offering for this luxury item, it wasn't at all pleasing to them to have to jettison the lot when the plane couldn't make it.

Because of this risk they stopped getting the fish out of the nets until the plane was actually flying overhead. Then there'd be a mad rush to empty the nets, pack the tins, and lug them down to the beach. In the meantime the pilot would have landed and walked up the bush track to help carry some of the load. There was always rush and tension, and always a race to beat the tide. Often take-off was delayed when there was a big catch to be brought out, and the tide would be far too high for comfort.

Carrying the tins was tough. Each man would bring two tins along the now well-worn path, and after a few hundred yards it was no light weight. The whitebaiters, at first Aubrey Bailey and Midgley, then George Mitchell, Midgley, and Dave Weckesser, later Eric and Dave, and finally Eric alone, had to learn by trial and error. Over the years they developed a technique that became highly efficient and scientific, and in the process learnt many facts about the life-cycle of the fish that had been little known until that time.

On the West Coast in some seasons the whitebait seem to start their run up-river earlier than elsewhere, and during 1948 they had a phenomenal run. In one eight-day period they netted 7,000 lb of fish, when there was nothing coming into the markets from any other source. Everyone, both pilots and fishermen, worked flat out; the fishermen even by torchlight in the early dawn and late evening clearing the nets and packing the tins to get it all away to the markets, always watching the weather, which in no time could abort the whole operation.

Then in the closing weeks of this season another aeroplane came to grief on the Big Bay beach. This was the Proctor ZK-AJY, piloted by Bill Hewett. We were still without radio contact, and it was inevitable that something like this would crop up again. Bill had again been delayed by bad weather, and the tide was on the change. In the softer sand which he was consequently forced to use the aeroplane tangled with some of the buried driftwood we all had nightmares about, and the machine nosed over, badly damaging the propeller. As in the previous season, the incoming tide and rough surf did most damage, and it was five months before we were able to salvage the aeroplane.

Bill was unhurt, but there was another furore in the news-papers. Luckily we had managed to locate him in a search from the Auster before a costly air Search and Rescue alert had been organised. We made two unsuccessful efforts to repair the Proctor and fly it out, but the elements beat us both times. We had to scrap the aeroplane, but contracted with Alec Black, owner of the launch *Alert*, to salvage anything recoverable. He took the *Alert* into Big Bay and made several trips by dinghy to the beach to bring out, with much effort, the remains. The awkward dismantled sections were loaded into the dinghy, manœuvered through the heavy surf to the side of the launch standing by, and laboriously hauled aboard. This was a severe financial blow, and not surprisingly the insurance companies were beginning to have their doubts about our kind of aviation. They hadn't much faith in aeroplanes in any case, even though we were always pointing out that, in proportion, the risks on the road were far greater. With this they couldn't agree, and we had to submit to a premium of 15 per cent on the capital value of the aeroplane, and $200 franchise.

After this little sortie the Post Office at last gave us permission to set up our radio network – one year and three aeroplanes too late – and now we wasted no time in getting our radios located and operating. We profoundly hoped that this would be the end of our run of bad luck; and certainly the flying risks on the Coast, particularly during the coming whitebait seasons, would be greatly minimised.

The equipment was already set up at our base at Frankton and now we installed Army ZCIs at strategic points: one in Midgley's hut at Big Bay, and another at Franz Josef Glacier. Later we had them at Martins Bay and at Hokitika Aerodrome. The sets were brought from the Government Stores Board and cost between $20 and $40 each. There was an additional cost in getting them serviced and fitted with crystals for the frequencies we were allowed by the Post Office. We obtained an ex-US AT5 transmitter and an Arc 5 receiver at a reasonable price, and in-stalled them at Frankton. This formed the nucleus of what was to become quite an extensive radio network, augmented later by two-way radio installed in most of our aircraft.

In 1948 seed-sowing was another job tackled by our firm for the first time. In early August I sowed grass seed for my late brother Clem Lucas at his property Moor Farm in the Clutha Valley. I'd always felt that there were great possibilities for aerial sowing, including tree-seed sowing, but although I discussed the latter often, I was never able to get anything really going in this line.

However the grass-seed sowing caught on rapidly. Barry Topliss fashioned a hopper out of an egg-pulp tin, and we did trial runs on the Frankton Aerodrome. Then on 19 August I did some more seed-sowing, this time for two farmers, Messrs E. Strain and A. Robins of Lake Hayes, not far from Frankton. September saw us sowing seed for Mr G. Jardine of Kawarau Falls Station and for farmers on the Crown Terrace at Arrowtown. Although seed-sowing from the air had been done overseas, I think this was the first time it was done commercially in New Zealand.

The Austers with their low stalling speed and manoeuvrability were ideal for the work, and although they have since been superseded by more modern aircraft they did a wonderful job and I shall always think of them with affection. Trevor Cheetham came with me on the first run to see that the seed flowed freely from our somewhat primitive hopper. Later, when more suitable hoppers were designed, the pilot could do the job on his own.

The most extensive aerial sowing with seed we did was for Mr R. W. Wightman of Winterslow Station in mid-Canterbury near Methven. He had approached the Minister of Lands regarding aerial seed-sowing, only to be told that it was considered impracticable. Later he had tried to interest the Ministry of Works in sowing it on a commercial basis. Government policy, though, confined this sort of work to Departmental requirements, but they did offer him advisory assistance. Consequently after these negative reactions he was pleased to hear about our seed-sowing efforts and promptly approached us to do the job.

District Soil Conservation officers of the Works Department arranged with him to observe the sowing and to peg out areas to test seed germination. It was planned to sow about 10 lb to the acre in an immense basin bounded by Mt Somers and the Old Man Ranges to the north and Mt Winterslow to the south. The area was known as Three Creeks, which had been burnt off a few weeks earlier in readiness for the sowing. I started to make the sowing in December 1948, with Topliss to help load the seed into the hopper, but a series of howling nor'-westerly winds made flying impossible, and we had to tie the aeroplane down to a blown-down tree to stay there all night in the teeth of the gale. The next day we went back to Queenstown until the weather improved.

When the weather cleared I returned to complete the job, working over Christmas and New Year. Major Jack Mac-Pherson of Lower Shotover, as my off-sider, helped load the aeroplane and feed the seed into the hopper. It was a grinding eight days of flying for me and loading for my helper, but at last the job was done. In all we sowed 30 tons of seed, which was contained in over 600 sacks, whose contents had then to be transferred to sugar-bags, and these in turn manhandled into the aeroplane, about 14 each trip. The loader squeezed in behind me and had a full-time job emptying the bags into the hopper, which accommodated only 50 lb of seed at a time. Any free moments were spent in making sure that the seed kept flowing freely. The average height at sowing was about 400 ft, which allowed an estimated spread of about 200 ft. The seed, Mr Wightman told me if I remember correctly, was a mixture of cocksfoot, ryegrass, browntop, white and suckling clover, with a percentage of yarrow and alsike. The time taken on the job was 42 hours 40 minutes flying, and the cost worked out at one cent per lb. Mr Wightman planned to keep stock off the country for 12 months, and to introduce bees to pollinate the clover.

It wasn't easy at first to interest farmers in aerial seed-sowing.

There were some forward-looking men keen to experiment, but many were cautious and parsimonious in their approach to the important factors.

For one thing, because it was being aerially sown, experimentally, they weren't confident of the results, and so "saved money" by using inferior seed with a low germinating factor. All too often someone would say, "I've got some rubbishy seed in the barn, you may as well try it from the air." What a waste. It didn't seem to occur to them that if they were going to pay for the aeroplane it would be better to sow a quarter as much pedigree certified seed and get twice the results. It was going to cost them far more to sow poor seed for no results. Those who used good certified seed could put out a third of the quantity over the same area, cut down on flying time, and get better results. I found that farmers who had insisted on sowing inferior seed would never admit that this was the reason for the low germination. They would be disappointed at the poor results, and pass on their doubts about aerial sowing to their neighbours and bias them against a trial. Soon, however, results justified our work, and we were sowing seed all over the province, for Phil Hunt at Mt Nicholas Station on the west side of Lake Wakatipu, and 30 tons for my brother Dick of Bendigo Station near Cromwell.

I was basically a farmer as well as an airman, and much of my thinking was orientated to any use to which aircraft could be put in the interests of primary production. It was clear to me that aviation could revolutionise time and labour-saving practices in agriculture as well as farming economics. Aircraft could greatly facilitate the rehabilitation of grasslands and tussock country, especially as it now seemed that the rabbit problem, if not licked, could be reduced to manageable proportions. If aerial seeding could be proved practicable, the eroded areas in the high country could be aided by aerial tree-seeding. This naturally led to the conviction that without suitable manure or topdressing, the success of seed-sowing would be considerably reduced. The very inaccessibility of most of the areas urgently requiring attention indicated that unless it could be done by air it would never be tackled at all. Higher costs and wages and a diminishing pool of suitable labour would see to that.

The hoped for contracts to do aerial tree-seeding did not materialise, but I was keen to get started on topdressing, as I was sure that there was even more scope for this than seed-sowing, and that anyway both could go hand in hand. I tried a small experimental sow for my brother Clem at Moor Farm. In 1948 too, the papers reported us doing topdressing at Lake Hayes, but I am not very clear on this point after so much time has gone by. There's no entry in my logbook for having done this, so Trevor Cheetham or Bill Hewett must have piloted the plane.

Our ideas were not original. Over a period of 25 to 30 years other men had seen the possibilities for agricultural aviation, in the USA in particular. Nevertheless it was only after the Second World War that topdressing as we now know it became widely practised.

I was keen to interest farmers in the possibilities of topdressing, and canvassed down around the Clutha Valley area, in South Otago, using Clem's place as a base, and driving about the district interviewing likely clients. In late January or early February 1949 I arranged for our firm to give an aerial top-dressing demonstration at a Young Farmers' Club machinery display at Pukerau. John Kilian, who was helping us out as a spare pilot, brought the Tiger Moth down and made a sowing. This served to quicken the interest in topdressing commercially. Orders began to trickle in and soon became a steady stream. Soon after, Clem arranged for a sow of super on his property, and invited neighbouring farmers to observe the results. I was giving a running commentary from the ground. During a lull I heard a farmer remark: "Fat lot of good that will do us, floating around up there," when he saw the swathe of super left by the aircraft still drifting down.

On the next round I asked the pilot to make a run over the crowd. He did this, and while everybody stood there, staring up-ward with mouths agape, a fine spread of super settled down on them, into mouths and eyes and over clothes. This gave the on-lookers some idea where the super really did get to, and must have convinced my doubting Thomas, as he later became a good client and supporter. We were soon doing more and more top-dressing as farmers began to see its potential, and also began to combine the aerial seed-sowing with the topdressing, dropping both in the one operation, which was a saving in time, labour, and flying costs.

In view of my early interest in the possibilities of the aerial sowing of super, it was always a great disappointment that although we were among the first in this field we didn't keep the lead. In anticipation of what I thought would be rapid growth in this type of aerial work, I made a survey of a wide area in the Hawarden and North Canterbury areas with one of my partners, John Kilian, who had by now joined the company, and John Patterson, of the stock firm of Pyne, Gould and Guinness of Christchurch. We canvassed a large area; the response was very good indeed, and a large amount of work was promised. How-ever when I returned to Queenstown I couldn't convince my partners that there was a big future in this for us, and so we lost the opportunity to really get on our feet. The orders we'd taken were turned over to an operator just going into the topdressing business and situated in the middle of this area. We did a certain amount of topdressing in Central Otago, but here there was not the same scope, nothing like the work offering in other parts of the South Island.

Soon of course Air Licensing had parcelled out areas for the numerous operators now starting up in business, so, even if we had wanted the work, the places with the most potential were now barred to us; and indeed, when we applied for topdressing licences at an Air Services Licensing Authority hearing in 1952, a licence was granted only on condition that we operated in one small area, and restricted ourselves to using only one Auster air-craft. There were three objectors at this hearing and they main-tained that we had other aerial work to keep us going and didn't need the topdressing work.

In any case by the end of 1949 the northern operators had come into the picture and topdressing was here to stay, to grow into the enormous industry it has since become. The surplus of wartime aeroplanes undoubtedly gave a terrific impetus to the rapid growth of the topdressing industry. There were plenty of DH 82s, or Tiger Moths, fondly known as Tigers. These were cheap and easily modified, serving as the workhorses of the industry until the more specialised aircraft made their appearance. We of course at this time were using our one Tiger, but the bulk of our aerial work was done with the Auster Autocrat, and later with the Auster Aiglet, until in 1956 we began to replace them with Cessna 180s.

The useful life of the Tigers was limited, and it was evident that more suitable types of aircraft would soon be demanded, preferably ones that had been especially designed for the work they were expected to do. The Auster company were on the ball and went to considerable trouble to design an aircraft especially for aerial agricultural requirements. So too did Captain Edgar Percival, designer and manufacturer of the Percival Gull and the Percival Proctors I to V series. Some of Percival's aircraft had put up terrific records from the UK to Australia in the 1930s. He now toured New Zealand interviewing all aerial operators, making plans to produce what he hoped would be the perfect agricultural all-rounder. He stayed at our home for several days, and went very thoroughly into the needs and requirements of the industry. He came up in time with the PC 9, which did a brief survey of New Zealand, and was doing work here when it crashed. It did not reappear on the New Zealand scene.

The Fletcher aircraft was especially designed for agricultural work, and became perhaps the best known aircraft for topdressing. The rapid growth in the use of Fletchers was given impetus when the NZ Meat Producers' Board instituted a scheme to assist the industry to equip with suitable topdressing aircraft, as it was becoming apparent that the work had outgrown the capabilities of existing machines. They made advances of 10 per cent of the cost of the new aircraft at a low interest rate and were instrumental in helping aerial operators re-equip with new machines until about 1956, when the scheme was discontinued. We didn't take advantage of this scheme as the amount of top-dressing we were doing was limited.

In 1950 statistics showed approximately 5,000 tons of super sown by air. By 1956 almost 50 per cent of the total superphosphate production was being aerially sown, and by 1960, when I left the firm the annual national total had reached 550,000 tons. By 1965 it had risen to 923,000.

IO

No Funny Business

IN ADDITION TO OUR REGULAR peak-period work we did a lot of miscellaneous charter and scenic flying. Fortunately Proctor ZK-APG was airworthy again, as the loss of the other Proctor was severely felt near the end of the year when there was much scenic flying offering. The tourist season was at its busiest from December through to April. In later years it stretched from November to the following May, and today is almost all the year round, with a slackening off only in June, July, and August. Even these quieter months are picking up, and the Queenstown area is looking forward to the time, almost upon us, when the tourist season will be buoyant the whole year round.

However the scenic flying was picking up fast, and we hired an Auster ZK-AQL from a Hastings owner to help tide us over the busy season. We had long passed the exhilaration experienced when we grossed our first $200 turnover for the day. At the outset, when we had small overheads, we had considered our continuation in business assured once takings exceeded that sum. But as with everything else, costs rose and rose, our plant increased and required more and more servicing, our facilities continued to expand, and there was continual pressure for more aircraft to cope with the demand for work. Staff needs grew, and the more revenue we earned the more we needed to pay out.

We tried again to get Rehabilitation loans, but where before our applications were refused on the grounds that our chosen work was too risky, now the reason for refusal was that we were already established in business, and that the aim of Rehabilitation loans was not to re-finance people already in business but to help ex-servicemen to get started up! So we couldn't win either way.

Now that we had established radio communication, our dealings with the weather became much easier. At last we knew what was happening on the other side of the Alps. Before, we were always getting on the wrong side of people who had been promised a flight to Milford; the weather at the Frankton base could be absolutely perfect, while at Milford and on the Coast generally the rain would be coming down in sheets. Our disappointed customers would accuse us of not wanting to fly, and to satisfy them we would make the attempt, but always after 20 minutes or so the plane would have to turn back because, as the pilot well knew, the cloud would be right down on the tops and the Pass clouded over. This might convince them, but it wasn't good business, and we always made a refund, which left us not only out of temper but out of pocket too.

Now, the on-the-spot weather reports were a great help in convincing would-be sightseers that the weather really was too bad. We were able to make the most of our aircraft potential, and the occasions were less when we might find all the fleet weatherbound at the glaciers while frustrated passengers were queuing up in perfect weather at Queenstown. At the Franz we had set up our radio-telephone in the quarters of Steve Sutton, a gardener at the hotel. Steve helped us in every way possible and was most hospitable, giving the other pilots and myself food, shelter, and generous hospitality on innumerable occasions. Later he joined the company and was employed as a man of many parts, loader-driver, gardener, and handyman, always hardworking and always cheerful.

The scenic flight to Milford Sound was proving most popular. Everybody enjoyed it. In those first years we flew very early morning trips into Milford, sometimes even at 5 a.m. This was often the best part of the day in the summer months – clear, fresh, and with little turbulence. Later, even by 10 a.m. there might be a deterioration of weather and visitors might miss the trip they most wanted to do. As this was before we built the

Milford strip there was no question of landing there and the flight was therefore a round trip, taking an hour and 15 minutes. Over the Milford Hostel, as it was then known, we would circle and drop a paper to Mr and Mrs Norman Berndtson, who managed the hostel, do the local sightseeing, fly over the Sutherland Falls, and return to Queenstown. We made short scenic flights over the Queenstown district, flying up the Frankton Arm, over Queenstown Bay and the township, on to Arthurs Point for a panoramic view of the Shotover Gorge and of historic Arrowtown, scene of early gold-mining days. This was a 20-minute flight and catered for the pockets of visitors, particularly family groups, who could not afford the longer trips. The most expensive flights were the round trips to the glaciers and Mount Cook. Anyone could go anywhere on a charter, and we flew people to Hokitika, Westport, Christchurch, Dunedin, and Invercargill.

Often there were ambulance flights with patients to go for specialist treatment to one of the main centres, although we weren't allowed to call them ambulance flights until late 1954, when we were able to induce the authorities to grant us a licence for this work. There were numerous requests for charters to out-of-the-way places, to service parties of scientists or prospectors wanting to probe the secrets of mother earth. Some were looking for oil, or gold, or scheelite, others for mica or semi-precious stones and, much later, uranium, when that fever was at its height. The ornithologists searched for rare specimens such as the notornis in the Takahe Valley, and the bird-watchers and photographers had their hides in various places, where they were surveying the habits of whichever birds they were currently interested in. They kept in regular contact with us, either for flights into certain areas, or for information on bird sightings.

We flew in parties of men to deerstalk, pighunt, or to shoot goat, wallaby, thar, or chamois. At times I flew a police party or the local constable from Whataroa into semi-isolated places where the construction gangs were – sometimes as a follow-up to an act of violence or robbery, but more often to nail a deserting husband or maintenance-dodger. There were many calls to fly out construction workers for medical treatment, or to some emergency on the domestic home front.

I met and flew hundreds of wonderful people. They were interesting to talk to, and I would have liked to have seen more of them; there were of course the minority that nobody ever wanted to see again. Later on when we had an aeroplane stationed permanently at the Franz Josef Glacier, catering for tourists and guests staying at the Hotel, there was a rare selection of odd incidents.

One day I flew over to the Fox Glacier airstrip, which at that times was about five miles down the road from the Fox Glacier Hotel, to drop off a couple of passengers. A Mount Cook Company bus driver asked me to stay long enough to take some of his 27 passengers on scenic flights. Two old dears wanted a longer flight over the Glaciers and around Mt Cook and Mt Tasman to have a good look at all the superb peaks and scenery. Neither had flown before, and they closely inspected all the controls and seating arrangements as they climbed in, watching in awe and some suspicion as I fastened their seat belts.

Both had broad Lancashire speech, and one declared: "Eh, Ah've never been oop before, lad."

The other said, "Ay, this is my first time too."

"Oh, well this is my first time too," said I.

"*Eee*, d'ye think you'll manage, lad?"

"Oh, I'll give it a go."

"Well, no foonny business now."

We took off into brilliant sunshine, with the Alps standing out crystal clear, and climbed slowly and steadily towards the Fox Glacier. There was hardly a tremor in the upper air and my two passengers were absorbing the view, commenting on the awesome depths below, the blue-green crevasses, and the virgin snow smooth like royal icing on a wedding cake, and at the same time keeping a wary eye on my manipulation of the plane. At 9,000 ft I folded my arms, content to view this primeval scene too. At once the more vocal of the two yelled in my ear, "Now don't you take your hands off that thing for a single instant!"

Just then, in a perfectly still sky the aircraft shuddered, and immediately the other leaned forward and tapped me on the knee, saying reprovingly, "Now, now, naughty, naughty!"

I tried to keep a straight face, but they were fun, even though confirmed back-seat drivers, and they really enjoyed and appreciated all they were seeing. This was one of the most satisfying things about scenic flying, when people really, genuinely, savoured all the grandeur about them. It made up for any little personality quirks.

One delightful Texan couple that I had already flown on some long charters were particularly appreciative, and on the final flight when we were weaving from side to side coming down the Franz Josef Glacier into the Waiho airfield, the wife, who had already shot many feet of movie film, continued filming madly.

"Say, honey," her husband protested, "you've shot off all your film."

"Ah don't care," she replied. "Ah'm jes' gonna keep on shootin'."

These were the sort of people who were out to enjoy the unspoiled beauty of a new country, and went away thoroughly impressed and satisfied with their trip. They are our country's best public relation types. The fact that their hotel may not have had quite the standard they expected did not spoil their visit. They were prepared to make allowances and to recognise the fact that these things could not be changed overnight, and that, as the volume of visitors increased, so too would the standard of facilities be raised. This was back in 1949 and the last 17 years have seen a marked improvement in the standard of tourist accommodation. Even after all these years these old friends still write and remember their "wonderful holiday in New Zealand, and that fantastic flight over the Glaciers".

The "negative" types made me impatient – those who read a book while flying over some of the most impressive scenery in

The exterior of Davy Gunn's hut which was used initially until the white-baiters built their own quarters. Davy Gunn (*left*) and Eric Midgely are watching the approach of an Auster

Auster ZK-APO being recovered from the Lammerlaw Range

Forestry stores freighted by Auster into Landsborough airstrip in 1948

First aerial rabbit poisoning by Popeye was carried out in September, 1948. Rabbit Board employees are filling the hopper of an Auster with poisoned carrot bait

the world, or were busy comparing what they were seeing with the superior splendours of "back home". One such couple chartered the Auster to fly from Queenstown to Milford Sound. Most of the not inexpensive trip was spent in criticising the scenery. We came to one of my special places where even I, who had flown past there hundreds of times, never failed to be enthralled, and I heard the wife whining: "Give me good old Taranaki any day."

Now I haven't anything against Taranaki, I think it is a delightful place, but I wasted no more time on that couple, just flew them the fastest and shortest way there and back. At times when I have had a particularly appreciative couple, it has been a pleasure to take them not only on the routine flight but to some of my favourite places, as a tribute to their discrimination.

Teasing the Aussies usually brought some retaliation. They were keen to enjoy new country, and seemed to delight in the mountain and alpine regions especially, but they like to leg-pull too, so I always tried to be in first to have them on. Flying up the coast I would shade my eyes and peer in an exaggerated manner out across the Tasman Sea.

Someone would be bound to say, "What are you staring out there for?"

I would look puzzled: "That's funny, it must be raining in Sydney."

They would look completely mystified. "How on earth can you tell if it's raining in Sydney?"

"Well, you Aussies are always skiting about your Bridge; it *must* be raining, because I'm darned if I can see it."

There would be derisive hoots, and none-too-gentle digs in the ribs.

Scenic and charter flying at the Waiho airfield and Franz Josef and Weheka airfield at the Fox Glacier provided most of our scenic work for the next few years, until the Franz Josef Hotel was burnt down for the second time and finally destroyed. After this the tourist work there fell off, and we operated more from Queenstown, Milford Sound, and Hokitika.

If tourist flying on the Coast kept us busy, so did the miscellaneous work at Frankton, on the other side of the Alps. We now had a few of our "firsts" behind us. Rabbit-poisoning, seed-sowing, supply-dropping, and topdressing. All this was now an integral part of our set-up. We also spotted for fires and dropped messages to firefighters. One spectacular blaze got away on Cecil Peak Station, on the west side of the Lake just opposite Queenstown, when track-cutters working in the Table Bay area let a fire spread after boiling their billy. Soon it was all over the mountain, and the station owner, Alex Burnett, and his men spent three days trying to check it. We dropped food supplies to the weary men on the mountain, and eventually to others when a general call for volunteer firefighters was made.

The Lakes District is a Mecca for photographers, amateur and professional, and we were often chartered by film units, New Zealand ones and overseas ones as well. Farmers increasingly employed us to spot for sheep and cattle in their high country, especially after heavy or late snows. We became popular with undertakers, who chartered us to make long flights the length and breadth of New Zealand, returning the bodies of those who had died far from their home places. The undertakers became "funeral directors", then, finally "morticians".

A severe spell of whooping-cough swept the district, and we were asked by some parents to help the sufferers. It was believed that a flight to 10,000 ft or so helped the children, and we did find that they seemed to gain relief in the rarified atmosphere – but only when the disease had reached a certain stage. If the parents could be persuaded to wait until the congestion was so critical that it prevented sleep, then the benefit was quite dramatic. Our own children had it quite severely, and I took them all up. I don't think, however, that any real scientific proof supports this belief.

Maternity trips were not uncommon, and for me always nerve-racking. I was asked to pick up a patient from Paradise at the Head of the Lake, near the Dart River, and to bring her down to the maternity hospital at Queenstown. She was quite matter-of-fact, and there was no sense of urgency, but the baby was born 15 minutes after arrival at the airfield. The next stork-flight was also to the Head of the Lake, at Glenorchy. It was a turbulent day, the District Nurse accompanied the patient, and there was every indication that the situation was very urgent. I thought we were going to make a delivery in mid-air, but at last I touched down at Frankton, and mercifully our passenger list had not increased. I was glad to see that taxi high-tailing it into the maternity home. The babe was not born until three weeks later.

In between badgering the Government for a Queenstown–Dunedin air service, we were trying to convince them of the need for and also the convenience of a regular flying service to Central Otago and Queenstown from the main city centres. The newspapers had been crusading for better services, and gave generous coverage to these problems, particularly the *Otago Daily Times*.

We tried to illustrate the potential for air-freight by intro-ducing an early delivery of newspapers to the more isolated areas, especially our own. In Queenstown the morning paper did not arrive until the bus got in at 6 p.m. or after, and unless personally called for it wasn't delivered until after midday the following day. The *Otago Daily Times* co-operated with us in an experimental delivery of 1,000 copies of their paper to Central Otago. The flight was made from Dunedin in October 1948, but the weather deteriorated, and Trevor Cheetham had to turn back after getting only as far as Naseby.

He dropped papers in lonely places and on farm homesteads, and made some deliveries to such country towns as Ranfurly and Naseby, but couldn't complete the scheduled trip. This paper run didn't come to anything, as the ground system wasn't able to adjust to ensure immediate distribution of the papers on arrival. Petrol rationing was still in force, and there was a great shortage of vehicles, so special deliveries couldn't be made. The papers had to wait to go on the Rural Delivery vans, and so any time gained in the air was lost because of ground facilities.

This season too we played with the idea of rainmaking trials. It had been particularly dry in some parts of Central Otago, and in North Canterbury the farmers were desperate for water. Experiments in rainmaking with dry ice were being carried out in the United States, Chile, and Australia, and Otago seemed one area that could benefit by the production of rain at required times. Bill Hewett was very keen to try out this idea, but we didn't try any serious experiments at this stage, as there seemed too many complications, such as producing rain exactly at the right time. Our financial resources were too shaky to run the risk of being sued for damages to some farmer's crop by producing rain at the wrong time for him.

About 1956, however, when Bill was operating his own firm he did make a trial. An Ettrick orchardist, Mr J. Hainsworth, supplied the dry ice, and Jack Humphries, then a pilot with Hewett's Aviation Ltd, seeded the rainclouds with it. According to newspaper reports, some rain was produced and the fruit-growers were encouraged. Ettrick was reported to have got a rainfall of 0·7 in., and Roxburgh 0·15 in., with somewhat smaller amounts in neighbouring areas. I don't think the experiments went any further, as the people sponsoring it had limited funds and technical knowledge.

We considered crop-dusting and aerial spraying, too, early in the piece, as we were anxious to tackle anything that would produce revenue. Here again Bill was enthusiastic, and although we did not persevere with any of this work, he himself carried on with it in his own company later. Our reasons against it were again financial: apart from the country within our area being too mountainous and cropping not extensive, there was too much legal responsibility and liability for damages if neighbouring crops were inadvertently damaged during dusting or spraying operations.

An enormous tussock fire got away in the Southern Alps, and although it seemed barren and unoccupied country, it was in fact part of a couple of high-country runs. Again the aeroplane proved its usefulness, spotting for fresh outbreaks, ferrying firefighting parties in to prevent the spread, accomplishing in a few hours what would have taken days on horse or foot. The time saved helped preserve feed, tussock country, and stock.

We established some of our earliest associations with members of the National Film Unit and with Bill Walker of the National Publicity Department, a happy association that has lasted to the present day. We did much of the flying for some of the best known documentary films distributed by the National Film Unit. There was Brian Brake's superb *Snows of Aorangi* and the late Johnny Hutchinson's *Four Ways to Milford*. There was Roger Mirams, who has now his own well-known film company, Don Oakley, Bob Lapresle, and Ken and Jean Bigwood, who took superlative bird photographs, and many others.

There were many times when because of the scarcity of hotel beds in Queenstown we had groups of complete strangers billeted at our house. Often we had to turn back because of weather, particularly before we had radio communication, and our passengers would find themselves without a bed for the night. Lorie made up beds at home and we did our best to look after them until the weather cleared. Most of them were a pleasure to have as guests, and were very appreciative of our hospitality. We made many lasting friendships over the years.

Access and transport facilities have certainly improved since 1948. Then, when Ken Myers, at the time a Field Officer in the Wild Life section of Internal Affairs, injured his hand while he was at the Fiordland Expedition's Stillwater camp, a series of transport manoeuvres had to be made to bring him out. Air transport wasn't possible because of the weather, and Alec Black of the launch *Alert* was radioed at Milford Sound for help. He made a fast trip to Caswell Sound, picked up the patient, and headed back through the night to Milford. From there the patient was transferred yet a third time to a car waiting to drive him through to the Gore Hospital, a long and tedious trip.

To foster interest in aviation and to try to make the public more air-minded, we instituted aerial displays and field days at Frankton Aerodrome, Cromwell, and Alexandra. Besides the displays and fly-pasts we had Brian Mussen of Auckland making parachute descents. Short scenic flights in between were the order of the day, and helped to pay expenses, and certainly stimulated public interest in flying.

Then we got the biggest freight-haulage job we ever had. This was to fly stores into Bluff Station, an isolated sheep-run 70 miles in from the Clarence in the Kaikoura Ranges. The usual way for the station to obtain their stores and equipment had been by pack-train. The pack mules were led over a rough 70-mile track into the homestead. We were told that it usually took the mule train two months to do the trip, at a cost of $240 per ton. In a few hours we had done the job for $104 complete.

It was hard work, and not without risk. The only landing place was on the edge of a cliff, and the Auster Autocrat was ideal for the job because of its ability to land and stop within about 60 yards. From the landing-field not far from the Clarence railway siding I made seven trips into the homestead. In all there were two tons of cargo consisting of a two-stand shearing plant, a generator weighing about 250 lb, 42 sheets of roofing iron, and a quantity of timber cut into 6-ft lengths to fit into the cabin of the Auster. I put in a full day of work loading the aeroplane at Clarence, then having to unload it at the other end. As a backload I carried out 1,800 lb of wool in 100-lb pocket packs, and 200 lb of rabbit skins and deer hides.

I had to land the laden machine on the edge of the cliff, and taxi uphill to a flat spot to unload. On take-off I taxied farther uphill, just as far as I could go, then took off into space over the cliff edge. It wasn't the most comfortable of landing-grounds.

II

'Bait and a Beginning

THE 1949 whitebait season was almost upon us, and we had been considering extending our activities to Martins Bay, just a few miles south of Big Bay. Since I had started flying on the West Coast, Martins Bay had held enchantment for me. I had flown down Lake Mackerrow, and over the land at the mouth of the Hollyford River countless times, inspecting it and wondering if it would be possible to make a landing there. I believe Arthur Bradshaw landed on a sandspit there in 1936, but by 1949 the spit was no longer in existence.

Martins Bay has an interesting and romantic history. In 1868 the Otago Provincial Council visualised a port to serve the West Otago areas, and the township of Jamestown was surveyed. It was planned to blaze a road over the ranges and through to Lake Wakatipu, but this never eventuated. Numbers of settlers moved in by sea, but few remained, and according to written accounts the project broke the hearts of most of those who did.

The Bay is about 15 miles north of Milford Sound, and a good 200 miles south of Hokitika. Access by land today is by a rough track over the ranges from Lake Wakatipu, or via Te Anau up the Eglinton and down the Hollyford Valley. The Hollyford River has its outlet at the mouth of Martins Bay, passing through Lake Mackerrow on its way. Big Bay adjoins to the north and is separated from it only by a rocky headland. Jackson Bay and the Arawata River are farther north still, 50 odd miles up the coast. Across the river, and to the south is the boat harbour, and near by the site of the Mackenzie homestead, ruined now and abandoned.

The locality has been practically uninhabited for many years, ever since the last Mackenzie left the Bay. There is fine scenery there, and a picturesque river, and a vast lake with some good beaches and superlative fishing. Enormous primeval forest covers most of the land and crowds thickly down to the water's edge, with occasional cleared spaces which have reverted to bush and secondary growth. The flats and basins of good country were for many years grazed by the late Davy Gunn, well known for his annual drives of cattle through from Martins Bay and Big Bay.

In 1927, 50 years after the collapse of the settlement, Davy took up a grazing lease and worked to establish cattle in the Hollyford. In 1936 he started a tourist business, escorting people about on tramping or riding tours. He kept the tracks open into Mackerrow and Martins Bay until about 1950, when the area was taken over as a National Park. Davy was then given an ultimatum to have all his cattle out by a certain date. The subsidy he had received for maintaining the tracks was withdrawn, and it became more and more difficult to get into Martins Bay. There were to be many attempts to drive all the cattle out over the next few years, but none very successful, and two lives were lost in the process. In recent years there has been an extermination policy of shooting the wild cattle still there.

Davy died in 1955, but at the time we were trying to open up this area he was still alive, a legendary figure, looking after his guided parties, rounding up his cattle, and making spectacular drives through to the market at Invercargill.

About six weeks before the whitebait season was due to open three brothers, Eric, Bert, and Cecil Mitchell of Ross, on the West Coast, were getting ready to go into Martins Bay. We had made an agreement with them to build an airstrip for the Auster and to prepare to whitebait there for the season. They travelled down to Hollyford in an 18-ft dinghy with the bare essentials for setting up camp.

On an earlier survey I'd made a trip on foot through bush and rough country into Martins Bay in company with Eric Midgley, who whitebaited each season at Big Bay, and a veteran hunter and back-country man, Lloyd Vient of Arcadia Station at the head of Lake Wakatipu. We tried to locate the best site, but the one we chose, although the approaches appeared better, proved to be unusable at certain times of the year because of water-logging. However, this was the site the Mitchell brothers worked on.

It took them 10 days to clear enough bush and rushes for the strip, and to drain the land, much of which was marshy and boggy. They were experienced bushmen, and when they thought they had cleared sufficient for a landing, one of the brothers tramped the 12 miles over rough bush tracks and through the tall rainforest, to the rugged coastline leading around to Big Bay. He kept to this, travelling on the beach wherever possible; when he reached Midgley's hut, after six hours, he called Queenstown on the radio-telephone and advised us that the strip was ready.

In three-quarters of an hour I had landed at Big Bay and picked him up. We flew round to Martins Bay, and low over the strip, but I found it impossible to land because of high bush and trees at either end. I throttled back the engine and glided low over the strip, shouting instructions for the further clearing of the site. Within minutes the men, who were among the leading competitors in woodchopping on the West Coast at the time, set to work again.

In a few days the trees had been removed and the stumps cleared away, and on 26 August 1949 I made my first landing there. During the next few days I made a number of trips, flying in fishing gear, provisions, and bush-felling equipment, including a saw bench and a motor to process timber, and materials for building a hut.

That season we flew out about 4,000 lb of whitebait, but for all their hard work and enthusiasm the Mitchells were disappointed in the results. Conditions were not nearly as good as those at Big Bay. The river was not as clear as the neighbouring Awarua; it was sluggish and slow-moving, and in some places almost 200 yards wide. By this time we had decided that our present strip was a problem one. There were several watercourses that were the cause of serious waterlogging, and so we planned to go in next year before the start of the whitebait season and hack out another one in a better position.

Meanwhile, Big Bay had to be serviced. Midgley and Weckesser had also been getting ready for another busy season. At first they'd had the use of a hut belonging to Davy Gunn, but by now they had completed a new, very comfortable hut nearer their place of work. It stood on the crest of a sand-dune, facing the glorious prospect of beach and coastline, backed by undulating sandhills and confronted by the pounding Tasman seas. It was built of punga logs, with malthoid roofing, and the inner walls were lined with sisalcraft, which kept the hut warm and draughtproof. All the materials except the punga logs had to be flown in, and any timber had to be cut into 6-ft lengths to fit into the cabin of the Auster. For the benefit of his spaniel, Peter, Midge built in a small swing door under the stove. Thus his dog could enter and leave at his own discretion, without giving entry to clouds of sandflies as happened every time the main door was opened.

Although it had been some time since anybody had flown into the area, we were not the first airmen, by any means. The late Captain Bert Mercer knew the coast well, having aerially pioneered the whole coastline since 1933–4. Arthur Bradshaw too knew Big Bay well, having been I believe the first to fly whitebait out, as far back as 1936. Bradshaw was famous for having flown the Tasman in a single-engined monoplane, and he was also the pilot of the fatal aeroplane crash at Big Bay in 1936, in which he himself survived although injured. Bill Hewett too had been freighting whitebait out of Big Bay the season before he went into partnership with me.

So Big Bay, although deserted for 10 months of the year, became during the two months' fishing season quite a social centre. Now that we were doing regular scenic flights into Milford Sound, there were numerous occasions when adventurous spirits begged us to take them into Big Bay. Because this beach airstrip was unlicensed for paying passengers, we had to be circumspect about who we took in. We usually took them in on a routine whitebait-freighting flight. A good many were professional photographers, newsmen, or freelance journalists. The whitebaiters became quite blasé about being interviewed, photographed, and filmed.

The fishing site used to be about a mile up the clear, tree-fringed Awarua River, which is tidal for a short distance. The source is not many miles upstream, nor very high above sea-level. During the annual run of the whitebait the Awarua is host to millions of these tiny fish, and the fishermen found that success depended on an accurate knowledge of the vagaries of the river and tide, and the habits of the shoals of 'bait so delectable to the human palate.

Whitebaiting this season held no fears. Everything went like a charm. There were no more accidents, and the daily radio schedules, giving weather reports and advising the condition of the beach, were a wonderful help. There was a great feeling now of confidence, and of being well-organised. We knew now how much 'bait was ready to come out, and the whitebaiters in turn knew that if the weather was right we would definitely be in on the low tide. The catch would be ready waiting on the beach, and we could be sure of delivering it kicking-fresh to the city markets. With no delay in loading, the pilot need have no more worries about rising tides. He just landed, helped load the catch, and took off as soon as possible. Everybody kept an accurate record of the tides, particularly the neap tides, as these gave us a longer interval when we could safely use the beach. At any other time we had only a two-hour deadline, either side of low tide.

The whitebaiters were gradually perfecting their methods and each season saw more and more efficient practices. Eventually there came a time when they installed live-boxes, a wire-gauze box kept afloat with the help of bundles of flax-sticks tied along the sides. In this way it became possible to keep the 'bait alive and on hand, even if bad weather delayed a plane for several days. With the ZCI radio set installed in the hut, the men kept a regular radio "sked" with Queenstown. They relayed their stores orders, and every evening at 8 p.m. they had a general call for information and news of the outside world. This helped relieve the sense of loneliness that sometimes oppressed them, especially when a prolonged spell of unsettled weather prevented an aircraft getting across to the Coast.

We flew in stores, mostly meat, eggs, groceries, bread, papers, mail, and medicine. Before we had the radio-telephone at the Bay we were often left with piles of stores and meat spoiling, because the weather was bad and the plane had had to turn back. Lorie would spend whole afternoons cooking up the meat in order to keep it edible until it could be delivered. There was still no electricity at the little cottage we were living in, and of course no deep-freeze or refrigerator, and so no way of preserving these stores, especially the meat orders. If the bread got stale it didn't matter, as the men usually toasted it, but Lorie often baked piles of scones or biscuits to give them a change of diet. Once it was 20 days before an aeroplane was able to get into Big Bay during which time Midgley and Dave Weckesser had to live off venison, fish and the inevitable whitebait.

There were occasions when medical advice or drugs were necessary. Midge always took his spaniel Peter in each season for company, particularly later on when he fished alone, and there was nothing too good for that dog. He loved whitebait and lived like a king; his bones were ordered regularly over the radio-telephone, as part of the stores order. Once he was burned quite badly and Midge called up on the R/T for medical advice. We contacted Airadio at Taieri, who located a vet and arranged for him to give advice over the air to Midge listening in at Big Bay. We obtained the drugs ordered from the chemist at Queenstown, and flew them in for the relief of poor Peter.

When the tide was low at Big Bay the remains of locomotives could be seen, an intriguing sight in this particular locality. They were the remains of a cargo from a Russian ship wrecked there in the 1870s. The beach was also littered with enormous boulders at the northern and southern ends, and I always meant to search for one which was supposed to have been seen decades ago, and to be of solid greenstone.

All through 1949 and until July 1950 we carried on our paper war with the Government and National Airways over air service licences, particularly for one to operate a Queenstown–Dunedin–Queenstown service. Both the Hon. W. A. (later, Sir William) Bodkin, MP, and the Hon. T. E. (later, Sir Thomas) MacDonald asked for consideration to be given to the proposed service. They pointed out that we already had suitable aircraft ready and waiting and, forestalling one objection that was raised by NAC, aired the point that the Corporation itself was operating single-engined Fox Moths south of Hokitika.

The official reply was that the "whole matter of licensing private operators is under consideration", tied in with another stonewaller that airfields up to the required standard would be necessary before any service could begin. We pointed out that the existing airfields needed very little to bring them up to standard, that we were prepared to do much of this ourselves, and that we had been offered help by the local people, who were just as eager to have a service established as we were to give it. We found that the Frankton Aerodrome had easy approaches with little fog or turbulence. Cromwell airfield was not ideal but would be good enough to start with, and there were alternative sites for development later. Alexandra had plans for a new site on a higher level away from the worst of the river mists which plagued the present one.

We were rather shattered when the Air Secretary wrote in reply to one of our innumerable applications advising that National Airways had appointed aero clubs to operate air charter, air taxi, and air ambulance services, and that these aero clubs would in most cases be the exclusive sub-contractors to the Corporation. On the face of this there was no hope for the private operator at all.

During this time and in support of our efforts there had been many applications and deputations from local bodies, chambers of commerce, and the fruitgrowers. This had been backed up by frequent representation from Opposition members, again Messrs MacDonald, Roy, and Bodkin. A sickly ray of hope was raised when the Government issued a statement saying that "while adhering to Government policy of a monopoly of the air network", they might be prepared to consider authorising, by contract, permit, and temporary authority, a private operation of air services in Central Otago. Public pressure had at last compelled them to admit that our area was long overdue for an air service.

But then, as a final nail in our coffin, it was announced that National Airways would establish their own service from Dunedin to Alexandra and return. However, they said, a private firm would be allowed to operate a feeder service to the scattered townships of the area.

For us of course this was absolute nonsense. There wasn't a hope of making such a feeder service pay. Operating such a service, and complying with the Authority's requirement that we use twin-engined aircraft, wouldn't even earn the licensing fees. Even the short leg from Alexandra to Dunedin that the Government intended to keep to themselves would be a losing proposition on its own, and needed the backing of other activities to carry it. In my opinion these short-haul airlifts in such scattered and low-population areas needed full utilisation of aircraft and complete flexibility; a basic timetable would have to be kept to connect with the main trunk connections at Taieri Airport. Unless we got the leg from Alexandra to Dunedin as well, it couldn't work.

I was disgusted when as an added smokescreen the authorities claimed that "inadequate aerodrome and route facilities, as well as weather conditions, precluded an extension of an air service to Queenstown". By this time we had built hangar space for three aeroplanes, had installed good refuelling facilities, and had an office and a waiting-room, plus good telephone and radio communication. Far better facilities, in fact, than were

present at the Alexandra Aerodrome even in 1959 when the
now defunct SPANZ started to operate into there.

As far as weather was concerned, we had found the percentage
of bad weather remarkably low. There had been few occasions
when we could not operate out of one or other of the two
practical approach routes. We usually came through the
Kawarau Gorge, but in rare fog we could get out in a straight
run down the Kingston Arm. If there were inadequate aerodrome facilities and weather, then this applied more to Alexandra, where aerodrome facilities other than an old shed were
non-existent and we often had to overfly because of fog on the
airfield; yet Alexandra was at that time apparently considered
adequate when the National airline intended to operate there
from Dunedin.

The fruitgrowers were especially concerned for a faster service
for their produce – apricots, cherries, and small fruits – as these
perishables were frequently spoiled by the long waiting periods
incurred during the freighting by rail and steamer service.
Growers were very fortunate if their produce reached the
northern centres such as Auckland in under three days.

The Minister of Aviation visited Central Otago, and was be-
sieged by deputations of people anxious for better air access. At
Frankton the Aerodrome Board, the Lake County Council, and
the Queenstown and Arrowtown borough councils, plus various
progress leagues, and Federated Farmers, presented a united
front in their desire for an air service. The Opposition member
for Wallace introduced the Frankton Aerodrome Board, who
expressly petitioned that the proposed NAC Dunedin–Alexandra service be extended to Queenstown. National Airways
had by this time announced their intention of starting the
service to Alexandra, but no consideration had been given to the
Queenstown end. A special plea was made that the development
of the air services and the tourist industry be fully pressed for the
Southern Lakes area.

At this, for us, historic meeting progress was made when the
Minister, while reiterating the Government policy on commercial

aviation, said that there "might" be one or two exceptions to their policy. One of these "could be Southern Scenic Airservices, as they were servicing the needs of a vast back-country area". He said "I have the greatest admiration for Mr Lucas and his partners in the splendid pioneering work already achieved"; and, "If the local company applied for a charter and taxi licence, it would be granted."

Memorable words, after the long battle lasting over five long years, first in my effort to get the Bristol Freighter Service going, and later any licence to operate anywhere.

But all was not yet straightforward. National Airways did some survey flights from Taieri, and on 12 December 1949 carried their first passengers, but later announced that the service would be restricted to air charter. There was little support for this, as a full load was required before the flight could be made. Any intending traveller would have to have sounder assurance than this that he could travel, and he did not want to be committed to paying for all the empty seats himself if he was to make his travel connections farther on. Tentative plans by National Airways to operate twin-engined DH 89s, better known as Dominies, were made, but trial flights confirmed the fact that it would be impossible to operate economically under the stringent requirements of Civil Aviation.

So now it was over to us, and at last we were ready to make the inaugural flight. We had progressed as far as obtaining an air certificate, but the licence to operate had not yet been issued. The opening date was planned for Friday 14 July 1950, but on that date I was still in Wellington trying to prod along various officials, and to tie up the last details. Thus it was the following Monday, 17 July, when the first official flight of the proposed twice-weekly service was made. Several inches of snow had settled on the Frankton Aerodrome, and this was unusual as there had been no snow of any depth on the airfield for several years.

Weather was poor, and the pilot, John Kilian, had to use the alternative route down the Clutha River via Beaumont.

Using the Auster for topdressing in 1949. Lake Johnson is in the foreground with the Remarkables Range in the background

Line-up of South-
ern Scenic Air-
ways early in 1950

Above: Leo White, Barry Topliss, Popeye, Stan Blackmore, and Trevor Sorenson posing before Stan's WACO aircraft

Right: Popeye helping to build a new
hangar. Cartoonist Chris Wren was
amused at Popeye's avowed fear of
heights

Originally our schedule was operated to cater for the local patronage, but after a long and losing trial, we found that we couldn't get a high enough load factor, and eventually organised our timetable to connect with the first NAC northbound flight, and to return to Queenstown after the last southbound one. This made it possible for passengers to get from Auckland to Queenstown in one day, arriving at the aerodrome at 3.30 p.m. They even had time to get up to the Coronet Peak ski field for an hour before skiing finished for the day. The service was welcomed by skiers and tourists alike.

Our usual flying time to Dunedin was about 45–50 minutes in the single-engined plane, a great improvement on road travel, which took a good eight to 10 hours, as the roads were then poor, unsealed, and terribly dusty.

H

12

Changes, Penalties, and Progress

JUST BEFORE THE START OF the season for whitebaiting in 1949, Bill Hewett got itchy feet. He wanted to go on a barnstorming tour around New Zealand and Australia. Topliss and I weren't too keen on this; we'd been working hard to build up a stable and steady business and to erase any public image of instability that may have been engendered by our earlier plane accidents and their accompanying somewhat alarming news headlines. So we couldn't see any advantage to be gained in this particular type of flying: we wanted to gain the public's confidence in flying as a safe and convenient mode of travel. Actually, we were older, and had worked some of the restlessness out of our systems; but Bill had still to do this, and he became bored when things were going too tamely.

During the year we had been finalising plans to begin private flying instruction at Cromwell. The residents were quite air-minded, keen to foster air travel, and so we came to an agreement to revive the Cromwell Aero Club. Some time had been spent getting the field, which doubled as a racecourse once a year, licensed. It wasn't the best of sites because of tree hazards at both ends of the strip, an awkward dip in the middle, and a hill at the north end, not to mention another hill sideways to the west, but it was serviceable enough, and would do for a start. In partnership with the Cromwell Aero Club and Cap Jardine, an air-minded farmer of the Remarkables Station, near Queenstown, we had bought a Tiger Moth. Bill was to be instructor, and was keen to get started. In fact the revival of the club and plans to instruct had been his idea in the first place.

However, this all fell through. We had discussed the pros and cons of the barnstorming tour, and the upshot was that Bill decided to pull out of the partnership and go on his own. Trevor and I were too busy to take on the instructing at Cromwell, and so Bill bought the interests in the Tiger Moth from the Aero Club, Cap Jardine, and ourselves.

Topliss and I bought out his interests in the firm, and Bill set out to start his tour as soon as possible. Shortly after, Tex Smith, who had flown with Bill the season before we joined him, came to Frankton to collect the Moth. Bill had persuaded him to return to flying, and he planned to accompany Bill on the barnstorming trip. Tex flew the Tiger to Rotorua, where Bill was holding a field day, but unluckily spun-in from 1,000 ft and was seriously hurt, with multiple injuries including a broken back, which kept him an invalid for many months. The Tiger was a write-off.

Bill carried on and made a successful tour of Australia, then returned to New Zealand to start up his own topdressing company at Mossburn.

Tex recovered, and when he was well enough to fly again was employed by Bill on topdressing operations for several months before joining our company in 1951. Bill's departure from the scene left us short of a pilot, and we chartered John Kilian of Christchurch to fly out the whitebait in his Proctor V.

While we were still pirating in this 1949 season, we persevered with applications to get licences to fly anything anywhere, as technically we weren't supposed to be in the air at all. The authorities of course were equally as determined that no operator except the National airline and the aero clubs should have any part of this ripe plum of emerging aviation waiting to be gathered.

Emergency trips kept cropping up. The isolated community at the Head of the Lake was very cut off; their only access to Queenstown was by lake steamer or charter launch, and in emergencies the time taken to get a patient to hospital could be fatal. We were the only aerial operator within 200 miles and it was unthinkable that we should not give our help when asked for it. Therefore it was a calculated infringement of Air Department regulations when we sent Trevor to the Head of the Lake on a mercy flight to pick up a Glenorchy resident who had suffered a fractured skull. He landed on the airstrip which was still unlicensed despite our repeated applications over the last two years, picked up the patient, and flew him through to Kew Hospital in Invercargill.

Within a few hours Trevor's pilot's licence was suspended, and a please-explain letter was received from Air Department. This grounding of Trevor was most inconvenient, as we were very busy and couldn't afford to have a pilot and machine out of the air. Then the Press got hold of it: there was a great fuss, and the licence was reinstated, but not without a severe reprimand and a warning that police action would be taken if Trevor offended again.

We made searches for overdue climbers and deerstalkers, members of tramping parties, and mountaineers marooned on some inaccessible face, suffering from exposure or frostbite or injury. During the ski season there was the usual crop of fractured limbs, involving numerous ambulance trips to fly patients back to their home towns. The need for a licence to operate an air ambulance was imperative, and so we were back to the tedium of making licensing applications: first for permission to transport ambulance patients and second, again to try to license the Glenorchy airstrip.

It was evident that we'd have to go on doing these mercy flights, and that there'd be a continuing need for them. The Coronet Peak skiing grounds were becoming more and more popular; each year more and more young people were participating in the thrills and spills, and inevitably there were injuries and requests for ambulance flights. It would be much more comfortable to do these legally and with the blessing of the Authority rather than lay ourselves open to disciplinary action every time an emergency presented itself.

Not surprisingly our application for an air ambulance licence to allow us to operate throughout New Zealand was refused.

I found myself increasingly called upon to do more mercy trips. A dangerously ill woman had to be transferred to the Dunedin Hospital. The roads were too bad and the trip too long for the doctor to risk taking her by road transport, and the local hospital hadn't the necessary facilities to treat her. The air trip took 55 minutes, and the up-to-date treatment at the bigger hospital saved her life.

Then came another accident, again at Routeburn, this time a woman and her 12-year-old son, injured in a car accident. I picked up the patients in semi-darkness in fast-deteriorating weather, from a bit of rough ground hemmed in by willows and by heaven knew what else. If visibility had been better I might have been too scared to risk it, but medical aid was imperative. There was barely room to take off, and the plane lurched into the air just clearing the willows. We staggered on until at last we were at a safe height.

Back at the aerodrome our office had made arrangements through Airadio for a flarepath to be laid at Taieri, but the weather closed in so rapidly that they decided to divert me to Invercargill. However, in the 20 minutes it took to fly down the Lake towards Frankton from Routeburn flying became so impossible that a continuation to Invercargill was cancelled, and I had to land in the dark at the Frankton aerodrome, with an impromptu flarepath provided by the headlights from cars parked by my wife and other members of the firm around the perimeter. Although this was another occasion when I should have had the whole book thrown at me for landing on an unlicensed aerodrome, flying after sundown without night-flying facilities, carrying passengers without being properly licensed, etc. etc., nothing happened. There had been too big a public outcry over the earlier one when Trevor was so severely penalised.

Then came the General Election, and a change of government ushered in a new look in aviation, transforming the embryo industry into something more positive and forward-looking. Suddenly private enterprise was being actively encouraged, and we felt full of hope, visualising a future free of the deadening frustration of having every application turned down as a matter of party policy. There were opportunities on every side, and a spur to progress that only aviation could give, and this only by the added drive of private enterprise.

By now we had increased hangar space and built proper refuelling facilities. We had a workshop with fully approved Civil Aviation Branch maintenance facilities, albeit we had yet to employ an engineer with the qualifications, to permit us to do our own certificates of airworthiness. We now had an office, a licensed radio installation, with our commercial network now operating between Martins Bay, Big Bay, Franz Josef Glacier, Queenstown, and Taieri. We kept regular radio schedules, at first on an as-required basis because we had to operate on batteries, but later a continuous listening watch once we installed the AT5 transmitter and ARC receiver and were linked up to the main power. We were obtaining reliable weather information and booking arrangements were much simplified. Our aircraft strength was a peculiar assortment – a Proctor I, an Auster Aiglet, and a Tiger Moth; we were down one Auster wrecked on the Lammerlaws, and one other Proctor written off at Big Bay. But in the year just past we had air-freighted 361,263 lb and flown 106,263 passenger miles. Fox Movietone had made a 20-minute feature on the activities of the firm, and we began to feel we had arrived. Then, miraculously, we were granted the licence to operate the non-scheduled passenger service from Queenstown to Dunedin and return.

John Kilian, whose Proctor V we had chartered for the whitebait season, came south again and decided to stay permanently, joining the company as a partner with Barry Topliss and myself.

Supply-dropping for the Wild Life Section took up an increasing amount of our time. I was away for weeks on end, dropping at Dusky Sound in far South Westland, or at Monowai, west of Nightcaps, a well-known mining area in Southland, and from there to Makarora near the Haast Pass, and all along the Southern Alps on both sides. I dropped into sites along the Tasman Range in the Nelson Province, in the Kaikoura Ranges in Marlborough, and at sites along the Clarence River, which runs between the Seaward and Inland Kaikouras. Fox Glacier was my base when dropping supplies into the South Westland alpine regions, and Hokitika for dropping north of Fox and all the way up in the Southern Alps. In the North Island the dropping sites were scattered through the Tararua and Ruahine Ranges, the Kaweka and Kaimanawa Ranges, and on up into the Urewera country. I operated from the Galatea Airport into the headwaters of the Whakatane River, and into the Ruatahuna area.

While doing a drop in the Makarora area near the Billy Creek, one of the tributaries of the Haast, I had an unpleasant experience. The weather was foul, but the cullers were a week overdue for a supply-drop, and we'd been waiting impatiently for the weather to clear. It wasn't good flying weather, especially in this sort of country which had more than its share of mountain hazards, but the chaps were getting hungry.

In the main valleys the weather seemed to have improved, but I found the small tributaries well fogged up. I flew down one trying to locate the dropping site, and saw it, momentarily, through a hole in the cloud, right below, with the sunlight shining on the exact spot. I put the Auster down through the hole, uncomfortably aware of peaks rising 8,000 ft on one side and 6,000 ft on the other.

I made the drop and started to spiral back up through the hole by which I had entered, and for about 1,000 ft it was OK, then suddenly the cloud closed in above and below me. I kept the Auster climbing in a tight spiral which was a little difficult without blind-flying instruments, unable to see a thing, and knowing that the surrounding clouds were all hard-core, that is, full of mountain inside! I heard the sound of another aircraft engine, then realised it was my own echoing back from what could only be solid rock. I straightened up and pulled the stick back, glimpsing at the same time snow-covered tussock and ice.

The tail-wheel rattled along on the hard snow. The Auster stalled over a bluff into opaque mist, and kept on sinking. Just when I was thinking that this was curtains for us we abruptly emerged below the murk – into the same valley.

I found myself flying along a side ridge with trees at the wing-tips, and the wheels just clearing the riverbed. There was no other way out, so we had to just keep on flying into the pouring rain with zero visibility. Then came a sudden sharp turbulence above a waterfall, and to my utter relief we broke into brilliant sunshine over the Haast River. Nobody was more thankful to see blue sky than I was, and that experience cured me of hard-core clouds for a lifetime; my chucker-out too, who was making his first supply-dropping flight.

It can pour, even on the east coast. Trevor Cheetham and I were camped at the Clarence Bridge, taking supplies into the Clarence Reserve and Quail Flat, between the Ranges. We'd been sleeping on straw in one of the Ministry of Works huts, and were beginning to miss the comforts of civilisation. It was Saturday morning, and the weather looked as if it was packing up, so the Forestry Field Officer supervising the drops ran us into Kaikoura for lunch and a couple of beers. While we were there the rain came down in buckets. It poured, and poured, and poured. The roads were blocked, and there were floods and slips throughout the district. We were unable to get back to camp until the following Tuesday, so it had been quite an ex-tended Saturday lunch. We were glad to finish this job before more wet weather delayed us further, and after finishing the backloading of mule-packs of wool and bundles of deer-skins, we headed back to sunny Queenstown.

There were frustrating days when it was difficult to make precision drops. Far below at a site in some secluded valley, a culler would put up a smoke signal to show us which way the wind was. I would allow for drift, but just as the 'chute was released a sudden change of wind would start the smoke drifting in the opposite direction, and the drop would fall off-target.

After a couple of misleading signals such as this, I would give up watching the smoke signals, finding it impossible in this type of country to anticipate the vagaries of the wind. Better to ignore any ground messages and rely on instinct and past experience.

The Forestry wanted a coal-drop made at a station hut on Mt Studholme, near Waimate. It was a very exposed place on top of the hills with no wood for firing, so besides supplies, coal had to be dropped in to the hunters. These men were employed by the Forestry to hunt wallabies in the Hunter Hills, where the animals, an importation from Australia, had increased to such proportions that they were now declared a menace, and as such within the scope of the Noxious Animals Division of the Forestry Service.

After an earlier drop a complaint was received that we were dropping the coal too far away from the hut. On the next run-in I tried hard for a good accurate hit on a closer target, and let more coal, one sackful loosely tied and placed within another, away on a free drop. I saw one man running for the hut, apparently afraid the falling sack of coal would clobber him, but the drop carried straight on, crashing clean through the roof of the hut and landing neatly in the coalbox at the side of the range, or so I was told later. It was closer than I had intended, but I don't suppose the occupants of the hut believed that; as for convenience – they could hardly ask for more!

Trevor wasn't very big, but he was tough. He had just finished supply-dropping in the Makarora and was preparing to return to Queenstown, but while swinging the prop it kicked back, smashing his thumb. It was a painful mess, and the cullers at the camp were concerned when he insisted that one of them swing the propeller for him. They were reluctant to do this, afraid that he might pass out during his solitary flight back to Queenstown. After some persuasion he agreed to one of them radioing our base to get somebody to fly him out. When Tex Smith got there Trevor was sitting on a log, apparently unperturbed, and it was the cullers who appeared to be most in need of attention.

One of my most painful jobs was the recovery of the body of a Forestry Field Officer, a good friend, Jim Kennedy. Jim had been shooting thar and chamois up in the Glen Lyon country, and was suffocated in an avalanche when a shot from his rifle started a fall. A party led by Max Kershaw, Field Officer from Queenstown, brought the body out to the head of Lake Ohau, where I had the sad task of flying it through to Dunedin.

During a spell of supply-dropping in the Ureweras, I struck a run of unsettled weather. It was really far too turbulent, but some of the cullers were overdue for supplies and the thought of men bushbound without supplies persuaded me to fly against my better judgement. It was very rough, with a high wind blowing. Discussing it with Rex Forrester, then Field Officer on the job, we decided to make the attempt. Rex would come to throw-out. The dropping site was at Te Whaiti, and I kept fairly high up because of turbulence over the site. Rex, on the signal, let the first package away and I did a circuit to see where it was going, but there was no sign of it; it had vanished completely. The mystery was solved when on looking upwards we saw it drifting about 30 ft above the aircraft. This was a pretty good indication that the ground was the best place for us on such a day, and we wasted no time getting back to the camp.

Sometimes cullers, perhaps new to the job and unfamiliar with aircraft, did not realise how lethal a package dropped from a great height can be. I always tried my best to drop accurately but sometimes wind and other conditions created vagaries difficult to correct. One culler, standing like an idiot right on the dropping site, was infuriated when a bag of flour fell so close that it nearly crowned him. He shook his fist at the plane, that much I could see, but it was only later that I heard he had fired a couple of shots at me with his ·303 rifle. One bullet, had it struck the propeller or the petrol tank, could have forced us down in some of the most inhospitable bush country in New Zealand. We were definitely not amused. One of the Field Officers heard him boasting of his effort in the local, and soon put him quite right on that score

Once, while dropping in the Ureweras, we experienced a different sort of sabotage. The site was near the headwaters of the Whakatane River, one of a number of dropping sites in country either heavily forested or covered with thick secondary growth. From a height the clearings were postage-stamp in size, sometimes not even that, just a column of smoke filtering up out of the bush. I would aim the drop where the smoke signals indicated, but there was a catch: some of the signals were decoys. Certain of the Maoris in the area had conceived the idea of putting up smoke signals of their own, well away from the official Forestry site, and presumably in the hope of receiving manna from heaven. I don't remember how the Forestry Service sorted that one out.

In the Southern Alps there was a different kind of pilferer. This was the kea, a protected bird in some areas. Sometimes while dropping into camps in the Alps the kea could plainly be seen, circling the package as it floated down attached to the 'chute. If there was no one on hand to receive the drop at once, there would be nothing left in a few minutes – the keas would tear open the packages in no time; cloth or canvas, sacking or cardboard, offered little resistance to these hardworking vandals. Checked only by the tinned goods, they would tear off the labels, and the cullers would never know whether they were opening a tin of canned beans or fruit salad.

For several seasons the keas had been causing sheep losses on some of the stations at the back of Queenstown. On this side of the Alps the birds are not protected, and so a farmer badly affected devised a way to get rid of them by poisoning. They are very inquisitive birds, loving fat and attracted to anything shiny, so he chartered us to drop, out along the mountain ridges, shiny, 4-gallon tins full of melted-down fat mixed with arsenic. I never heard what results he obtained.

Apart from Forestry dropping there was always work coming forward annually for the alpine and tramping clubs. Some of the earliest drops I made were for them in 1947. Also at this time we were rock-salt dropping for farmers. We made airdrops for private and professional wallaby hunters, goat-shooters and deerstalkers. In the Alps the hunters sought red deer, thar, and chamois. In the far south-west in Fiordland they hunted moose and wapiti. We made supply-drops for them in the Caswell and Bligh Sounds, at Monowai, Makarora, the Landsborough, the Olivine, on Mt Dobson, and Mt Aspiring, and farther north at Waimate, to mention only a few. The Southland section of the NZ Alpine Club engaged me to drop prefabricated hut materials into the Moraine Creek Valley. We dropped aluminium walls, other prefabricated materials, and cement. The only loss was a bag of cement, which rolled away from the target into a creek. On another occasion we dropped a prefabricated hut on to Wrights Col on Mt Earnslaw, at the head of Lake Wakatipu.

We dropped food for climbers and surveyors, and supplies for the Fiordland expedition at Caswell Sound. There was much work to be done for clubs and private parties over the next few years. Occasionally a drop was made on the wrong site, and this was embarrassing for us and inconvenient for the recipients. It wasn't always easy to know exactly where the correct site was. We had only the instructions of the leader of the party to go on; these might be verbal or written, and sometimes accompanied by a photograph or a map with the site marked on it, often roughly and none too clearly, in pencil or smudged ink. On the site, the target might be marked out with a white cloth laid out, or newspapers held down at the corners by stones. If there was snow, Condy's crystals were often used as a marker.

I had arranged to make a drop for wapiti hunters who had drawn lots for a block to hunt in Fiordland. This part of the world is a maze of crags and cliffs, of almost impenetrable rain-forest, of lakes or tarns on the tops, and knobs, one exactly like another, with masses of streams meandering off in all directions, all making dropping-site recognition a challenge. I was supposed to drop on a site at a place called Oilskin Pass. The place looked identical with the written instructions I had been given, but I dropped it on the wrong saddle. It took days for the party to recover their supplies.

I hated making a mistake like that. The joke has been on me ever since. The men concerned never fail to inquire, "Hey, Pop, can you tell us where the Oilskin Pass is?"

Regularly we dropped coal supplies into the Quinton Hut, just below the Sutherland Falls, on the Milford Track. At first we did it with the Auster, but in later years after we had bought the Dominies we could drop several tons in a short time. The hut was connected by telephone with the Milford Sound Hotel, and when I returned after making another drop at Quinton, I found a telephone message promising me a bottle of whisky if I could drop a bag of coal on the target, a sheet laid out on the ground. I tried very hard, and on the third attempt hit the edge of the sheet. The bag rolled on to it, rolled up in it, and rolled off with it. However this wasn't good enough, so on the next trip I tried even harder, and scored a direct hit, and was advised that the whisky was coming up.

It was near New Year's Day, and I thought I would return this compliment. I wrapped up a bottle in corrugated cardboard until it looked the size of a 25-lb bag of flour, and on the next scenic flight over Quinton let the parcel go. I saw it disappearing into the bush, with somebody running madly after it. I had fears for his safety, and gave the whisky up for lost, but back at Milford Hotel, I was amazed to hear that the bottle had been recovered intact – and also, to my relief, the eager sprinter.

13

Accidents and Fatalities

ON 16 AUGUST 1951 I landed the Auster Aiglet on a sandspit at Milford Sound. The engineer and I were making a survey, seeking a suitable area to build an airstrip. Soon after 8 a.m. we had finished our inspection, and on the invitation of Mr and Mrs Norman Berndtson were enjoying a wonderful breakfast of fresh blue cod at the Hostel. We handed over some supplies, and the mail and newspapers we had brought in. Our earlier contacts with Milford Sound had been by telephone and radio, and remotely by dropping a newspaper whenever we were in the area, as a goodwill gesture.

We had met the Berndtsons, however, when we were salvaging the Proctor off Big Bay beach when Alec Black had eventually to bring it round for us and offload it at Milford Sound. We were to receive much kindness and hospitality from Lin and Norm over the following years, and will always remember Cussie, Mr Berndtson senior, a vivid and colourful personality, a grand old man who for many years skippered the tourist launches at Milford Sound.

The only suitable place for a landing strip was on a river delta within 300 yards of what was later to become the New Zealand Tourist Hotel Corporation's new Milford Hotel. We had high hopes of forming this into a permanent licensed strip for use most of the year, particularly, we hoped, during the winter months when the road to Milford was closed and snow and avalanches blocked the Homer Tunnel. We were planning on co-operation from the Tourist Department for tourist bookings and from the Ministry of Works who, we hoped, would hire us a bulldozer, as they were expecting to have one in the area within the next few weeks.

The Milford scenic flight had not lessened in popularity and it seemed logical to try to land the tourists there. It would make a vast difference to the fuller utilisation of the existing accommodation which had to shut down in the winter months because of the closing of the land routes. Winter was often the driest period of the year, and in our opinion the best time for scenic flights.

We returned to Queenstown later in the morning confident that a suitable strip could be built, and delivered the mail to the Queenstown Post Office, just 30 minutes after leaving Milford – an improvement on the several days it usually took to reach Queenstown from Milford via Invercargill.

By now Steve Sutton, who had been employed at the Franz Josef Hotel, had joined our staff, and he worked for weeks at Milford, clearing the site. We hired the Ministry of Works bulldozer to prepare the ground, and Steve used a 15-ft tree trunk with a 3-ft girth to help level the surface. He towed this behind a tractor, and finally effected consolidation by the use of a roller, made from a 4-ton ship's buoy. The strip, at first only 550 yards long, was situated on the delta of the Cleddau River, where it flows into the Sound, and by May 1952 it was completed.

I made the first landing on 1 June, elated that now we could operate a regular service, bringing in mail and provisions for those constructing a new wing for the hotel. Immediately we began planning for the extension of the strip to bring it up to the standard needed to land a twin-engined aeroplane, as we were by now negotiating to buy two Dominies from the National Airways Corporation.

Air access made a big difference to the hotel; it allowed a longer season, and relieved the very real sense of isolation experienced by the permanent population during the long winter months. Before the aeroplane became commonplace the sea gave the only access during the winter.

Trevor Cheetham made the official inaugural flight on 11

June, when the first official mail was flown out, and there was a great demand for first-day covers. We began regular freight carriage and later, when the remodelling of the hotel was completed, we transported many hundreds of tourists in and out, and backloaded with fresh blue cod. For some years Civil Aviation allowed only the approved pilots of our company to land there, and this stipulation held good until in 1956 the Government took over maintenance of the strip, extending it to 1,000 yards and licensing it as a public airfield.

The year 1952 was a terrible year for mountain accidents, fatalities, drownings, and lost trampers. We dropped supplies to a climber sheltering in the Aspiring Hut, suffering from exposure and frostbite. And Gavin McIntyre, then a scheelite miner but now a safari operator at Queenstown, was seriously injured when he was crushed by his falling horse as they both rolled over and over down the steep slopes of Black Peak, at the head of Lake Wakatipu, where he was scheelite-mining 6,000 ft above sea-level. Word was got to us by telephone, and we picked up our local doctor, Dr M. F. Soper, and flew him to Glenorchy. In climbing boots, and with an eight-man stretcher party, he climbed non-stop to the injured man, gave him what temporary relief he could, and returned again, non-stop, to the waiting plane. The patient was desperately ill, and we wasted no time getting him back to Frankton and into the Lake County Hospital.

Emergencies such as these were always cropping up, and Dr Soper had another gruelling trip when he went to the assistance of a man who had broken a leg and been exposed to terrible conditions almost at the Double Cone, near the top of the Remarkables. Our district has been lucky always to have had general practitioners who have been prepared to go to such lengths to succour their patients.

There was a disastrous fire on the forested slopes of Mt Titiroa, in Fiordland, and somebody else needed urgent medical attention on a glacier. Another climber had to be rescued from

Right: Awkward cargo was this wapiti head shot by Dr M. F. Soper of Queenstown, which was flown out from Milford Sound by Auster

Below: Popeye in 1956 with the Franz Josef Glacier in the background

The business of getting a 'bus to the farm to start a daily tourist trip from Queenstown presented several difficulties

Right: Cecil Peak homestead with one of the peaks of Cecil Peak in the background. Popeye and his family took possession in 1960

Below: Popeye and Lorie dressed in style for celebrations marking the Wakatipu centenary

the Mt Cook area, at considerable personal risk to the rescue party. We dropped messages, fire-spotted, did aerial searches, and dropped supplies of food and medicine on many of these occasions, and the public was loud in its criticism of the cost of the air Search and Rescue operations.

Then two young women from Oamaru went missing in the Martins Bay area. They had been members of a tramping party being guided through the Lower Hollyford. On this morning in January the party, accompanied by a guide, had set out on a tramp to the hut at the head of Lake Mackerrow. The two girls became separated from the main party, and it was not until the others reached the hut at 7 p.m. that they were missed. The guide went back along the track, but came to the conclusion that they had become tired and had turned back to the hut at the Bay.

That night heavy rain, such as only the Fiordland area can produce, fell: in all, about 5 in. in as many hours. Creeks which had been dribbles become torrents. The party searched at first light, but were cut off by high streams. The Pyke River had risen to dangerous levels, but some of the party managed to get through to Deadmans Hut two days later, to get word out. An air Search and Rescue sweep was delayed because of the terrible weather, with low cloud and mist, torrential rain and gale-force winds. It was now three days since the girls had gone missing, and hopes were fading for their safety, as they had hardly any food, or clothing suitable to withstand such conditions.

Notwithstanding the weather I managed to make a preliminary search, but without much hope, as the dense bush precluded any real chance of a successful sighting: this was ground-party work of the most gruelling kind. I landed at Martins Bay with cross-winds gusting severely, and left supplies for the party of searchers who were mobilising as quickly as possible. I had as a passenger Sergeant Matheson, the relieving police sergeant at Queenstown, who was to supervise the operations.

Two boats were shipped round for use in getting up into

1

Lake Mackerrow. Two doctors, both house surgeons at the Dunedin Hospital, luckily were in the area and freely offered their services. We had never ceased to be thankful that we had been allowed to instal the radio-telephone at Big Bay and Martins Bay, and now this was invaluable in keeping hourly schedules between the searchers and the outside world.

During the next few days an intensive search was maintained. The weather was atrocious. The greatest difficulty for the searchers was to establish some point on the track where the girls might have met misfortune, as by now it was fairly certain that they must have been swept away while trying to cross one of the swollen streams – in which case the bodies were probably by now swept out into the Lake. The task of finding them was therefore formidable. The Lake's depth is estimated at 40 fathoms, it shelves steeply at the edges, and the water, glacier-fed, is bitterly cold. Experienced bushmen said that in these conditions bodies seldom rise to the surface.

We kept an aeroplane on standby, but there was little an aeroplane could do except ferry in supplies for the weary men whenever the shocking weather permitted. Then a few days later the body of Miss Lenore Algie was found in the Lower Hollyford area, in a deep pool at Six Mile Creek, on the track leading back to Martins Bay. Some personal possessions indicated that the girls had been drowned trying to ford the creek. Most of the searchers were confined to the hut until the next day, when the weather lifted enough for me to get in and fly out the body, and some of the party. The rest came out on foot, leaving six volunteers to continue the search for the other poor girl, Miss Daphne Williams. The inquest was held at Queenstown, and all hope was abandoned of finding Miss Williams alive.

While this search was going on another emergency had cropped up in the Te Anau area. A climber, Phil Dorizac, had fallen over a 50-ft cliff. His companion helped the injured man until he could go no farther, then left him, sheltered as much as possible in a tent, while he went for help. The same gale that was hampering the searchers at Martins Bay raged here too, and some of the men from this search were called in to rescue the climber who by now had been almost a week waiting for help to come.

Several weeks later the body of Miss Williams was found by Davy Gunn, and once again I went in to recover it and bring it to Queenstown.

All these happenings accentuated the need for a better way to effect rescues. We needed something more manœuvrable than conventional aircraft and I was convinced that a helicopter was the answer. Apart from the scope for profitable work there seemed to be in other fields, on a purely humanitarian basis the helicopter could save lives, and also the public purse, if used on rescue work.

For some time I had been in correspondence with an operator of a helicopter outfit in Canada. He had started off with one machine and now had a fleet of 15, all working flat-out. The possibilities for our country seemed limitless. The only drawback for us would be the lack of population to create sufficient work to make a helicopter economic. Nevertheless, I became one of a syndicate of six who planned to import a Bell 47DI helicopter. The change in Government policy towards private operators was now very evident: the Minister of Internal Affairs assured us that U.S. dollars would be made available when we had finalised our arrangements for capital, and the Minister in charge of Civil Aviation promised co-operation if any difficulty was experienced in procuring a machine from overseas. One of the prime movers, and one with the most faith in the venture, was Doug Shears, a businessman from Timaru. He was indefatigable in gathering facts and figures for the project. The finance was guaranteed, and the goodwill expressed by the Government was encouraging. It was pleasant to know that for once we were being viewed with approval.

The Bell 47DI, according to the makers, would carry a load of 700-lb or two stretcher-cases. The price would be $ (U.S.)

18,000 plus $ (U.S.) 1,200 for spares, shipping costs, the cost of conversion and travel for the pilot and engineer. We figured it could be fully occupied in wildlife work, spraying, and general duties, besides being always available for mountain rescue and mercy occasions, and so we settled down confidently expecting to reach some finality within a few weeks.

In the meantime our Queenstown–Dunedin–Queenstown service was proving popular, and as it prospered we made tentative plans to purchase a Nordyn Norseman, a single-engined aeroplane capable of carrying six passengers in luxury conditions. However Civil Aviation requirements demanded twin-engined aircraft in our area, and so we started negotiations to buy two Avro Ansons which were for sale at the time. One was a Mark I, ZK-BCL, and had been used extensively in the Empire Air Training Scheme during the war. We bought it from the Air Force quite cheaply, and got it airworthy enough to fly it to our base at Queenstown, intending to use it for freighting. However Civil Aviation regulations required us to do so much to it before they would approve it for work that we never put it in the air. It stood parked on the perimeter at the Frankton airfield until in 1960 it was destroyed by fire.

In 1952, with the purchase of the other Anson in mind, we contemplated the provision of some sort of regular service to the Chatham Islands. The settlers there were greatly in need of better access, and we thought we might be able to do something about it. We discussed the Chatham Island question with the Government who showed interest. The RNZAF flew one of my partners to the Chathams to make a survey, but in his opinion there was no practical way in which we could operate the service on a paying basis, and so reluctantly we had to abandon the idea. I personally was disappointed, as I'd have liked to provide better or at least swifter access to this community who so hardily put up with the inconveniences and frustrations of life on an island far removed from the mainland.

In the meantime the Anson was ready for delivery and I went to Tauranga to test-fly it and bring it back to Queenstown. The

RAF roundels had not been removed, and I had a twinge of nostalgia when I saw them, which stayed with me all the way back to Queenstown. This aircraft was a Mark XII, and in much better condition than the one we had bought off the RNZAF. We had intended to use the other for freighting, but this one was perfectly adequate for passenger service work. She'd been used as a VIP aeroplane in Australia to transport the then Governor-General, the Duke of Gloucester, on official visits about the country.

She had only 650 hours up since new, and had been especially designed for feeder-line services, with a cruising speed of 150 mph. Registered ZK-AXY she was a good aeroplane and deserved more use than she had had. With the acquisition of this machine we had to extend the airfield at Frankton. The existing length was quite adequate in our experience, and in all our use of the plane we never at any time had need to use any more of the runway than that, but Air Department were adamant that a longer runway was necessary and refused to license the aerodrome for an Anson until we had complied with this requirement. We were compelled then to rent a strip of land from a neighbouring farmer at $10 a week just for the privilege of looking at it.

The Anson served us until the purchase of the Dominies from National Airways. After that we found the Dominies so much cheaper to run that the Anson was taken off passenger work completely, and we were happy to be able to relinquish the renting of that perfectly useless strip of land.

We put in another application for a licence, this time to operate a feeder service from Dunedin to Christchurch with intermediate stops at Oamaru, Timaru, and Ashburton; we thought this extension would tie in well with our existing Queenstown–Dunedin service and help to put it on a paying basis. At the licensing hearing we were granted only the leg from Dunedin to Oamaru. The section on to Christchurch was refused in favour of another operator who had applied for similar rights. This restriction made the proposed feeder extension uneconomic; however, we started the service, only to abandon it after several weeks' trial as a losing proposition.

By this time the two National Airways Dominies became available. NAC withdrew them from the Dunedin–Invercargill run and we took delivery, using them on the Queenstown–Dunedin service in preference to the Anson.

Many months had gone by since our applications to bring in a helicopter had gone forward, and once again a fatal mountain accident spurred us to further efforts. This was one more occasion where, had something more versatile than a fixed-wing aeroplane been available, the victims could have been recovered quickly and successfully and the needless loss of other lives been avoided.

Some Wellington trampers were 12 days overdue in the Matukituki Valley area. We were helping in search sweeps, hoping to have some good news to give to the ground search party based at the Aspiring Hut. Then Air Department sent out an RNZAF Harvard to join the search. Shortly after entering the search area, contact with the Harvard was lost, and we were diverted from the main search to look for the missing aircraft. It was not until 5 p.m. that Trevor Cheetham, flying in an Auster with Tex Smith spotting for him, located the Harvard, crashed in an inaccessible place about 4,500 ft above sea-level near the Dart Saddle. They reported their find and later returned to drop medical supplies and a stretcher to the rescue party who were approaching the scene of the crash.

The one survivor, Flight Lieutenant Aubrey Bills, although shocked and with an injured leg, did what he could for his companion before starting on a grim two-hour trip back to the Aspiring Hut for help. The pilot, Squadron Leader G. C. N. Johnson, who had received multiple injuries, apparently died soon after his companion had left him, and the search party could do nothing except recover the body.

This accident once again confirmed the need for a helicopter and again we pressed for permission to import the Bell 47DI. During all the months of trying to finalise our plans we had collected a mass of information, and our application to the Licensing Authority had gone forward, but no finality could be reached until the publication of the Government's *Helicopter Report*. The Director of Civil Aviation had obtained direct from the Bell Corporation all the information we could need, and had made it available to us.

By this time however the original machine we had envisaged had been superseded by the 47G, similar in performance but with range and endurance increased by a third. The price also was in excess of our previous calculations. The new type would cost $ (U.S.) 38,280, considerably more than our earlier estimates. A year's supply of spares was quoted at $ (U.S.) 8,000 and it would cost a further $ (U.S.) 3,000 for special tools for maintenance and repair work, and $ (U.S.) 800 for dismantling and crating the helicopter for export to New Zealand. On top of this we would have to budget for a pilot and engineer to go to the United States to do a conversion course.

After several more months the way was made clear to go ahead and import the helicopter, but by this time there were so many demands on the time and finances of our company that we withdrew from the syndicate. Another member, an aerial operator, withdrew for the same reasons, but the rest pushed ahead with their plans and eventually they got the company operating successfully.

14

Odd Jobs

INEVITABLY THE WHITEBAIT SEASON came round again. The previous season had seen the departure of the Mitchell brothers, and the installation of three new men at Martins Bay. As our first airstrip had proved unsatisfactory during the wet season, we had spent some weeks hacking out another, farther away. This proved a considerable improvement on the first, but was still not by any means ideal. However, it was the best we could produce considering the limitations of terrain, and became our permanent strip. We eventually extended it to 616 yards with a width of 50ft.

I spent a week over there with two helpers, Tom Robertson of Queenstown and Bill Dennison, a farmer from Lower Shotover. We had obtained permission from the various owners of the property to clear land for an airstrip but they stipulated that we cut out no virgin bush, and in this we were lucky, as this particular area had been one of the earliest cleared by the ill-fated settlers of the 1870s and it had only reverted back to secondary growth of scrub, flax, and rushes, and straggling saplings with some scouring of old riverbed and many swampy patches. We spent every day clearing away this rubbish. My companions made light work of it. Tom was powerful, though one-armed, and as good as two men. Bill was like a one-man bulldozer – his progress could be followed by the uprooted saplings and pungas torn out by the roots. He had the strength of a bull, and when his hands, which were like hams, grasped a clump of flax or scrub, it came out by the roots and was tossed aside.

Davy Gunn had given us permission to use this hut near by and its shelter was welcome though somewhat primitive. It was built of logs cut out of the bush, and comprised a small annex where Davy did his cooking, and one large bunkroom, which had been used to sleep up to 42 people. Two enormous double-decker bunks, 6 ft wide, lined both walls. They were built of the same timber as the hut and the occupants just lay in rows in their sleeping-bags. There were no mattresses, just poles with the knots and protrusions hardly trimmed off, and overlaid with masses of springy fern leaf. Those without sleeping-bags slept in their clothes, rolled up in blankets, and there was no provision for division of the sexes.

The fireplace was of typical West Coast design, the chimney set at one end of Davy's "kitchen" being of corrugated iron, while inside, above the open hearth, hung the smoke-grimed hooks from which were suspended the big black iron cooking-pots. Although the kitchen floor was lined in the bunkroom it was just packed dirt, and often messy when a group of trampers staggered in wet and dripping out of a torrential downpour.

That rain had to be seen to be believed. Bill used to say that the drops were so big that a chicken-netting roof would have been sufficient to keep them out.

Davy Gunn was as tough as old boots, and expected no less from his tramping parties. He provided no frills and they loved it. He rode his horse and led a packhorse with the rations, and the rest had to walk. He wasted no time on a day's journey, and believed in a big feed in the morning and another one at night: Stopping at midday to boil the billy was for sissies.

The menu varied little – mostly venison or beef stews. At various places along his regular route he had food caches stored, some in primitive safes, others, such as venison or beef, hung up after he had shot and butchered the animal, in his larder – a branch in a high tree. We used to fly him in sacks of peameal, much of which he used to thicken his stews, and flour, with which he made his own camp-oven bread.

Bill got friendly with a fantail. Somewhere it had lost its tail but that didn't halt its activities. It would follow Bill around all day, alighting as near as possible to him, even on his shoulder, or settle to watch him, bright-eyed, when he stopped to rest on a log or to eat a meal, and in between with practised efficiency it would catch for itself edible insects and big fat blowflies.

Apart from the food we had brought in with us there was plenty of natural food about if one had the time to forage for it. We ate venison, and the lake and river teemed with beautiful rainbow and brown trout. It was possible to spear flounders down at the beach, and find crayfish around the rocks.

The tall bush was alive with birdlife: bellbirds, tuis, fantails, tom-tits, and hundreds of wood-pigeons. Occasionally a black swan would float majestically down the river, and sometimes the white heron would fly gracefully across the lagoon, or stand in silent contemplation on the riverbank.

Every now and then a crashing in the undergrowth marked the presence of one of Davy Gunn's steers. An old white bull haunted the Bay; often coming out on to the airstrip to graze, and often when coming into land we would have to buzz the strip to clear it of deer or cattle. Once, when Trevor was almost on the ground, three wild horses bolted out on to the strip and straight into his line of approach. He opened up the throttle and staggered off again only just in time to clear the horses and dodge the trees at the far end of the runway.

With the initial clearing finished Bill and Tom and I went back to Queenstown. A few days later I went in again with another party, and we spent six weeks clearing the ground of the remaining stumps, rushes, and other debris, and draining off water, of which there was more than enough.

The new strip was still only suitable for landing the Austers, and we could get them off with a 500-lb load of 'bait. We never landed the Proctors there. This season the new whitebaiting party came in again. They were a little disappointed in the results, although by this time living conditions were far easier, and with full radio communication now, operations were safer.

Stores were flown in regularly, and the Martins Bay men kept up
a daily schedule with Midgley at Big Bay, and much of the loneliness was alleviated.

This season and in later ones other whitebaiters moved in to
fish the Hollyford, at the mouth of the river. Bill Hewett, now
operating on his own account, planned to use the old, abandoned airstrip. His was a terrific feat, flying in a bulldozer in
sections, using his Aerovan. He had an ambitious plan to build an
all-weather airstrip, and to put in some of his own men to ex-
ploit the whitebaiting. Another aerial firm installed men at the
fishing sites too, and soon the place began to get somewhat
overpopulated. Something about whitebaiting brings out the
argumentative side in people, and at times when the fishing
wasn't too good tempers flared between the rival camps over
quite trivial matters. Isolation breeds further tensions, and it
wasn't always a happy group we found when we went in to
collect a load. During these two seasons relations became very
strained between the two main factions.

Other aerial operators contemplated whitebaiting there, but
the signs of strife must have put Bill Hewett off, for we saw no
more of him for a while, and the remains of his bulldozer are
still there.

The year 1956 saw a culmination of some of the ill-feeling
that had been building up at the fishing sites at Martins Bay;
the one operator who had established himself there besides ourselves had conceived a plan to develop this part of the world as a
tourist venue for hunting, fishing, and sporting groups, with the
emphasis on overseas sportsmen.

Our first warning was when we received a signal from Air
Department advising all aerial operators that complaints had
been received of unauthorised pilots and aircraft using the airstrip against regulations, and that any offenders would be
punished. We of course were using the strip, legally, and intended to go on doing so. Bill Hewett told us he had been
warned off, as did Freddy Adams of Adams Aviation. Neither of
them had any title to the land that the airstrip was on, and so

they decided to retire gracefully. The other company did not need the strip as they were operating amphibians.

When we had first landed there in 1948 we had obtained permission from the landowners concerned to have our strip on parts of their land. Now we made haste to have this renewed in writing as quickly as possible – and only just in time. As the last written confirmation was received, we had a communication from Air Department, warning us that our licences would be suspended because we were persisting in illegally using the strip. We had pleasure in replying that we were legally entitled to land there and would go on doing so, and sent proof of this.

On our next trip in we found our group most uneasy. Our men were concerned about a whisper on their grapevine that the "other side" were planning to put up a high aerial at the end of the strip for better radio communication – an installation which would block the approach and prevent us using our strip. Whether this was true I never knew, but it produced another burst of defensive action in which I promptly bought the vital 50-acre block of land that protected the approach.

On the next trip in, our beleagured men had had a wheeze on the grapevine that a trip-wire was to be stretched across the strip to prevent us landing. This seemed a bit far-fetched, but for the next few trips in we kept a sharp lookout before coming in to land. However, nothing like that ever eventuated, and whether it was the result of fevered imaginations and the bickering between the rival parties, I never new. The trouble simmered down, and we ceased getting signals from Air Department triggered off by complaints from others.

At Big Bay we never had any trouble because only one licence was issued for fishing sites during the time I was flying into there, and so no rivalries developed. Martins Bay had several sites, and as the fishing wasn't as good, and often the season poor, quarrels were more frequent. By this time we had nothing to do with the fishing side of it. In the early days we bought the 'bait direct from the fishermen in order to stay within the law, when we had no licence to carry freight for hire and reward; but once we had obtained our freight licence we had no need to do this. Now we were purely carriers chartered by the fishermen to fly out their catch, but we had a moral obligation to look after them too. So, apart from freighting in their stores and white-baiting gear, we took in mail and papers and medical supplies. We kept regular radio schedules, delivered messages and made toll calls, and contacted wives and relatives when required.

Having bought one block of land more or less by accident I was keen to get more, thinking that it would be good to get one for each of my four sons. Martins Bay holds a fascination for those who go there regularly. My wife and I spent some time locating owners to find that most of the land had reverted to the Crown. Some of the owners had not been traceable since 1901. Many of our letters were returned through the dead-letter office, and the few remaining owners were not keen to sell for sentimental reasons.

About 1963 the Crown decided to issue a proclamation closing any surveyed roads in the area and vesting the land in the Crown. Objections were to be lodged within three months, and the land was to be included in the Fiordland National Park. We lodged our objections.

By now the whitebait "war" had died as suddenly as it had arisen; we went about our business, using the strip when we wished. We took more and more fishing parties in, and hunters; the lake and river abounded with superb fish, and trout caught weighing up to 10 lb are no rarity. (Once, during the whitebait fuss, I had flown in a surveyor to find the pegs in one of the blocks of land in dispute, and while he went about his work my wife and I went fishing, and I caught a limit bag in 20 minutes.)

Martins Bay wasn't the only place to get involved in the silly season. Farther north at Paringa, Little River, and other places on the Coast, there were annual arguments and squabbling over sites, and the alleged moving of nets. The local fishermen re-sented outsiders coming in and trying to usurp their traditional sites, but the use of the aeroplane and newspaper publicity each season had encouraged people from as far north as Hamilton to come south for the whitebait harvest. The Whataroa constable had his work cut out keeping the peace and inspecting the rivers in his dual role of policeman and official fisheries inspector.

The late A. Blechyndon who was air-freighting whitebait out from the Paringa and other areas got involved in the feuding. The season swung into gear with reported complaints of torn nets, boats set adrift, and attempts by rival factions to prevent the 'bait getting out in time for the early markets. The police-man had to make repeated day-long journeys to the trouble spots.

Blechyndon, according to newspaper reports at the time, found his tail-wheel slashed. Later he had to force-land on a shingle strip at Paringa, and on inspection found his fuel tank had been spiked with sugar. He force-landed again before he got back to Hokitika, with sugar again blocking the filters. Tom Harris, engineer for West Coast Airways at Hokitika, inspected the tanks, and estimated that at least 3 lb of sugar had found its way into the petrol tank.

With so many fishermen working elbow to elbow, site-jumping and arguments occurred daily, but once the season was over all the animosity seemed to dissipate.

Besides the now regular flights and landings in at Milford Sound, we had started experimenting in fence-dropping, trying to find the most efficient way to drop materials without damage to posts and wire. For some time we had been dropping hut materials and lengths of dexion for hut-building, using wing-racks, and we adapted this method for the fencing.

The greatest drawback in those earliest attempts was the excessive damage done to the coils of wire on impact. Then this was practically eliminated by the simple and inexpensive device of coiling the wire on to halved tar-drums. I did quite a big drop for my brother Dick at Bendigo Station near Cromwell, on 24 March 1953, which was quite satisfactory, although damage to materials was still too high, about 15 per cent. Over the years techniques and packing methods improved, and the material considered suitable for this type of fencing was reconsidered from time to time, providing in the end an efficient alternative to packing out the materials on horseback, or by Land-Rover, or lugging it manually hundreds of feet up the mountainside.

There was no end to meeting interesting people. They were always popping up with letters or messages of introduction. One evening when I answered the telephone a voice with a marked German accent said, "Is that you, Herr Lucas?"

"*Ja, mein Herr,*" I replied, thinking it was some practical joker.

"Dees ees not fonny," came the reply. "I vas told for to look you up."

I hastened to make amends. He had been a German night-fighter pilot, and an acquaintance of mine had suggested he should contact me when he got to Queenstown. I arranged to meet him for a couple of pints at the local, and we exchanged reminiscences about the war. It came out that he and I had been flying in the same sector at the same time. I had been taking part in attacks in the Hamburg–Bremen area, and he had been lying in wait for just such as me. He asked me what I had been flying.

"Wellingtons."

"*Auf!* Dey vas easy. Dey vas *no* trouble to shoot down." He shrugged and spread his hand expressively.

"Well," I said, "that may be so; but you didn't get me."

We had another drink. I told him I had been flying Mosquitoes during D-Day.

"Don't talk about dose tings," he interrupted. "Dat's vat shot me down!" He showed me scars across his arms and chest to prove it.

After he had recuperated he'd been posted to a Junkers 52 transport squadron, and found himself flying champagne from France to the Russian front. "For der morale, you know."

They always flew low, he said, because of the champagne

cargo. One day the weather was exceptionally bad, and they had to climb 10,000 ft. "All der corks blew off like machine guns. All ve had left vas der smell! Der Kommandant, he vas very angry."

This fellow was still keen on flying, and came to the airport every day to see what was going on. He seemed an unshakeable type, though somewhat arrogant, and knowing that he was travelling by bus from Queenstown to the Hermitage, I decided to shake his calm. At the time I was rabbit-poisoning in the Lindis Valley, and crossing the main road frequently. I kept watching the down road towards Tarras for the bus. A dust cloud heralded its approach, and I timed myself to meet the vehicle as it was coming out of a cutting at the bottom of Cluden Hill. I completed the poisoning run, and then beat the bus up at ground-level, Stuka style, thinking that might shake him out of his complacency. A few days later I met the bus driver.

"How did your German passenger react?" I asked.

The bus driver grinned. "He never even looked up from his book!"

Towards the end of the year I took an Auster up to Wellington to finalise a certificate of airworthiness. Somebody inspected the propeller and promptly condemned it, making some scathing comment on the condition of the leading edge which had been repaired but which, in my opinion, was still absolutely safe. However they were insistent, and before I left a reconditioned one was fitted, and I threw the old one into the back of the plane.

The following morning at first light I was happily on my way flying out across Cook Strait, heading for Nelson, where I had a passenger to collect. I stayed the night in Nelson and the next day took off for the Franz Josef Glacier. By the time I was over the Buller Gorge the weather had begun to deteriorate, and soon it was like pea soup, raining hard, and with visibility down almost to tree-level. Just on the other side of the Gorge, near

Four sons (*left to right*), Charles, Martin, Richard, and David in Collins Burn Valley, Cecil Peak Station.

Members of a Crusader Camp held annually at Cecil Peak, Crusaders use shearers' quarters and cookhouse facilities

A recent picture of the author helping in the kitchen

Some of the tourists enjoying a break at Cecil Peak

Earnslaw pulling in to pick up logs. *Moana* can be seen at the wharf

Cronindon, the Auster was suddenly racked by a terrific vibration. Hurriedly I switched off the motor and began a long glide, searching all the time for some suitable place to land. Below was a rough, close-packed jumble of bush and ridge, with just a few small clearings dotted along the riverbanks.

I managed to put the Auster down on one of these, miraculously without damage to the plane or my passenger. We rolled to a standstill only feet away from a deep ditch; there were fallen trees, old logs, and piles of decaying sheep-bones; there were stones and rocks scattered among the uneven humps and tussocks. Any of this debris could have put us on our nose in an instant, but we'd missed the lot. We walked over to a building which proved to be O'Malley's, the local pub. I borrowed spanners and returned to the Auster to remove the "good" propeller, from which 6 in. of tip had snapped off. It didn't take long to replace it with the one that had been thrown contemptuously into the back seat.

There was no room to take-off, and I had to enlist the aid of some of the spectators, who had turned out when I force-landed. They were very pressing in their invitations for us to stay the weekend. The Reefton races were on, and they thought this was a good enough excuse for anybody. However I was anxious to get home before the weather really closed in, so had to decline.

They were kindness itself. We had to take down a fence before I could get enough room to take-off. What a job! Every post had a "foot", a piece of four-by-two nailed across the bottom of it. Many hands made quick work of clearing away the dead sheep, bones, logs, and clumps of blackberry and tussock that littered the ground. An enormous totara tree was right in the centre of the "runway", and I had to do a complicated semi-circular take-off to avoid it. I hadn't much cash on me, but turned out my pockets and gave the chaps all I had for a shout, thanking them for their efforts, and apologising for the fact that I couldn't replace the fence.

They assured me that I needn't worry and so, with my passenger still game to fly with me, I opened the throttle, dodged

K

round the totara, and was soon airborne, heading south once more. The weather got steadily worse, and we were weatherbound for the night at Franz Josef. This wasn't any hardship however as we were made welcome by Dick and Dawn Brooks, who were managing the hotel then. I was able to get a message over the R/T to the aerodrome and my family, to relieve their anxiety because I was overdue. Weather next day was still foul, but there appeared a clear patch, momentarily, just over the Waiho aerodrome, and I got out of there fast before it closed in again. Sometimes we could be weatherbound at the Franz for days, and it was best to snatch the first opportunity that presented itself. Poor visibility, rain and head winds forced me to fly the long way home and soon we were considerably overdue on our ETA.

Back at Queenstown my wife was concerned when the ETA had stretched to over two hours overdue, but our engineer, whom we always accused, rightly or wrongly, of being more concerned over the welfare of the plane than the pilot, assured her that all was well. She hadn't told him who my passenger was, knowing he would probably be in a flap if he knew, and she took a perverse delight in studying his reactions when his sister stepped out of the Auster.

Out of the blue I received the Coronation Medal; the first I knew of it was when I received a registered package. I'd seen a list of the recipients in the newspaper, but hadn't read further than the headlines.

Almost at the same time there came a signal from the Commanding Officer, Group Captain Theo de Lange, of RNZAF Station Whenuapai, asking me to send up to the station copies of my footprints. I replied somewhat less verbosely, "ROGER, WILCO, POPEYE". In anticipation of the Royal Visit in 1953 the Whenuapai CO had decided to refurbish my ceiling footsteps, which had become obscured over the years.

My wife, remembering the condition of underclothes and sheets after previous hilarious nights in the mess when ceilings had been the target, insisted on taking precautions. First she

opened up a Kornie box and laid it blank side up on the laundry
bench, then she ran hot water into the sink, shaking plenty of
powdered soap into it. Between us we blackened the sole of my
feet with shoe polish, and I carefully left the imprint of my feet
on the Kornie packet, stepping straight off there into the sink of
water to save any mess. You could have heard my yell all over
Frankton: she'd forgotten to add any cold water. Once she had
made sure I wasn't desperately harmed, she thought it a terrific
joke and helped me wash my feet – not, let me hasten to add,
from any sense of wifely duty but just to make sure that no shoe
polish was left to mark her nice clean carpets or linen.

After this involved business we read the telegram again,
properly this time, and found out that the Air Force wanted not
one, but a duplicate set of footprints. So back to the Kornie
packet, and the shoe polish, but this time no boiling water; I
made sure of that. The footprints were duly used as guide-lines
for the redecoration of the originals, but the Queen never went
near the Officers' Mess when she visited the station.

The weather was beautiful, and people were queuing up for
flights to the West Coast. A ring came through to the office: a
VIP was being sent out in a chauffeur-driven car to be taken on
a flight to Milford. No, he didn't want to share a plane with
anybody else and would we look after him well?

Soon the car arrived and the driver, smart in uniform, peaked
cap and shiny black jackboots, got out, opened the rear door,
and stood rigidly to attention. I stood in diplomatic expectancy,
waiting to greet the distinguished visitor. However, he continued writing in his notecase, ignoring such as me. After a
while he recapped his pen, an expensive gold monogrammed
one, and placed it in his breast pocket. He folded his notepaper,
reached for his briefcase, opened it, and packed away his
writing materials. I felt mesmerised as he withdrew a beret and
shut and relocked the case. He took off his Homburg, dusted it
meticulously, and laid it along the back of the seat. Then with
the aid of the rear-vision mirror, he adjusted the beret at just

the right angle on his head. Never once during this performance did he indicate, by word or look, that I was waiting to receive him. At last he left the car, and gazing somewhere to my far left, grunted a guttural "Good morning".

I half expected him to click his heels, give the Nazi salute, and cry "Heil Hitler". The chauffeur continued to stand, heels together and stiff as a ramrod. My passenger gazed in amazed disparagement at my little Auster, complained that it was too small, and said that the perspex windows were scratched.

I thought, "This is going to be a beautiful trip!" In the Auster there is a little tassel on the side of the cockpit, placed there for passengers to grip in turbulent air, or to use to lever themselves out of their seats. Before we were even airborne I saw the diplomatic hand reach for the tassel and clench it until the knuckles showed white. Then I knew what to do. I gave that important gentleman the most exciting flight anybody could hope to have. We flew in and out of valleys, skimmed mountain-tops, swooped down virgin snow slopes, sideslipped round corners, surveyed the Sutherland Falls and Lake Quill in tight turns, and all the way there and back he sat tense and upright, looking neither to right nor to left, and never once relaxing his grip on the tassel.

On landing back at Queenstown, there wasn't a great deal of conversation, and he had to prise his hand away from the tassel.

During the year mumps swept through our household, and the children had hardly got over it when I contracted it. A delivery had been made by a carrier of about 20 fruit trees and as many shrubs and I'd promised my wife, days before, to dig the holes and help to plant them. They were still unplanted when I was ordered to bed, and so it was that two unsuspecting friends, an airline pilot and his brother-in-law, calling on me in the expectation of a pleasant and convivial evening, found themselves instead planting fruit trees by moonlight.

While I was in bed with mumps, Merv Harper, of what was

then Harper and Adams Aviation Co., had the bad luck to spin in into Lake Hayes while on topdressing operations. There was an urgent call for somebody at the aerodrome to fly over the lake and drop a Mae West lifejacket to keep the ditched pilot afloat until a boat could reach him. Unfortunately all our pilots were away on aerial work, and Steve Sutton, our loader-driver-cum-general-factotum, climbed into the old aerodrome truck and rushed down to our house to see if I could possibly make the flight.

I wasn't in very good shape; I had a fever and could walk at hardly more than a shuffle. In the special circumstances my wife didn't feel she could prevent me flying, but she didn't approve of me rushing off without waiting to dress. I had hurriedly pulled a dressing-gown over my pyjamas, and with two days' stubble on a horribly swollen and misshapen face, I was a sorry-looking sight. Steve, in a bit of a flap, threw the gears of the truck about with such abandon that the gear-box was stripped and we were left stranded in the middle of the road. I crawled out and started to hobble up to the aerodrome, 500 yds away, but luckily a Department of Agriculture truck was passing by, and the driver picked me up and drove me post-haste to the Auster, which was waiting, ticking over, with the door off, ready for the rescue equipment to be thrown out when I was over the site. It was bitterly cold, and flying in thin pyjamas with the cabin wide open to the elements wasn't particularly pleasant.

After this comedy of errors, when I flew over the spot I saw the hapless pilot being determinedly rescued by the Dennisons, father and son, of Lake Hayes, who had put out into the Lake in a very leaky dinghy and were now bailing for dear life as they made for the shore. Needless to say, pilot and rescuers reached the shore safely, and as for me, I went back to bed with an increased fever and a relapse, and not much sympathy; mumps, being such an unromantic complaint, caused me to be nothing more than a mild figure of fun to all except the doctor and my immediate family.

When salvage operations were started to recover Merv's plane, nobody seemed to be able to locate its exact position. Eventually I re-enacted the flight, trying to drop the marker where intuition told me and trying to block out from my mind where reason was insisting it should be; in fact it was eventually recovered only a foot or two away from where I dropped the marker.

One of the more unusual loads I carried in the Auster was an enormous wapiti head, the property of our local doctor, Dr M. F. Soper, who was a keen outdoor man and spent much of his spare time deerstalking or bird-watching and in bird-photography. He'd been hunting in Fiordland and had chartered a plane to fly him back to Queenstown. He had procured an excellent head, and wanted to bring it out with him.

At first I thought we would have to leave it behind, as there seemed no way of packing it into the Auster. However he made it clear that if the head didn't go neither did he, so I took a second look at the problem. I had brought a topdressing Auster as this was the only one free at the time, and the hopper took up most of the rear space. The only possible way to carry it was to settle the head in the top of the hopper and leave the antlers sticking out over the top of the fuselage. Then I secured the whole thing by tying it firmly with rope down over the leading edge of the wing and on to the strut. We reached Queenstown without incident although with the antlers sticking so far up into the slipstream, a good 15 mph was knocked off our cruising speed. It certainly looked a bit odd, too.

15

New Ventures

IT WAS NOW 1954 and we were once again entangled in more air licensing hearings, this time opposing National Airways, who wanted exclusive rights to operate in the South Westland area. They were showing an $8,000 a year loss on this section and wanted scenic and joyriding rights to boost their returns; we opposed this strongly.

Ever since the formation of our own company we had been operating on the West Coast, and until the Franz Josef Hotel was burnt down had stationed at least one aircraft there on a semi-permanent basis. The South Westland area at this time was very isolated, under-populated, heavily bushed, and poorly roaded; the only really convenient access for some parts was by sea or air. The Licensing Authority, in fact, refused to deprive us of our licences for this very reason, on the grounds that the public would suffer from a reduction of services, and also that it wasn't in the public interest for the National Airways to have a monopoly.

Although we sympathised with the Corporation and knew that their losses had been consistent, we certainly didn't think they should get relief at our expense. We did agree at this hearing to relinquish our licences to operate into Westport in their favour, but we needed the Haast for charter flights, and for the use of the Anson in picking up crayfish tails and other freight. We used the Okura strip for deerstalkers, freight, and chart and the Weheka and Waiho strips were in regular use for supply-dropping, charter and scenic work, and alpine parties. To lose any of these areas would seriously upset our routine.

We were already in opposition to National Airways at Franz Josef. Only recently they had spent $1,200 on extensions to the airfield, and now had their own hangar. We had used this building in previous years but were now excluded from it and had to park our aircraft out in the open. I must confess that in fact we continued to use it when there were no NAC aircraft in the vicinity.

Feelings ran a little high, and over long and protracted hearings our respective lawyers harangued each other, probing for weak points in evidence. This dragged on for months, until it was at last resolved when we again started negotiations to buy the South Westland section from Hokitika to Haast from National Airways.

This move would solve many difficulties. Earlier in 1952 we had started negotiations with NAC to buy the section of their service from Hokitika to Haast. In 1947 they had acquired this section from the late Captain Mercer, who had pioneered air services on the West Coast since 1934 with his company, Air Travel NZ Ltd, but they had found that the Hokitika-Haast leg showed a continuing loss. I felt we could reverse this trend because of our other activities, and it would tie in very well with our scenic flying at Franz Josef. Charter flying and the promise of topdressing and supply-dropping would further increase revenue.

With the scenic, charter, and joyriding rights we already held, we could improve the economics of the scheduled run and give greater flexibility to our operations both on the Coast and from Queenstown. Both parties would be satisfied.

In the earlier negotiations we had in fact made a down payment of $1,000 to the Corporation in anticipation of concluding the deal. Also with this sale in view, the Corporation had not opposed our applications at that time for licences and renewals of licences, just then coming up at a licensing hearing. For various reasons, one being the destruction of the Franz Hotel by fire, thus removing our main source of revenue from scenic flying, the sale fell through. National Airways were very decent in refunding us our deposit less legal expenses, as they would have been within their rights in retaining it.

Naturally after this they felt we had obtained our licences and renewals under false pretences and advised us that they were applying for a revocation of them. Hence the protracted hearings of the previous months. Now, however, with negotiations again under way, and eventually being brought to a satisfactory conclusion, any ill-feeling was soon dispersed, and the Corporation were as helpful as possible, whenever our interests and theirs did not conflict.

Meantime on the other side of the Alps life was becoming busier and more complex. Besides the two Proctors, the two Dominies, the old Tiger Moth and the Anson, we now had six Austers constantly busy on aerial work. During the season four of them were continually on rabbit-poisoning work. Life was ruled by the weather and the rabbit boards. Trevor would be stationed for weeks at Kurow, and Tex and I working elsewhere for different boards. Competition too was getting fierce; more and more operators were starting up, and some of them had distinct advantages over us, as they owner-operated only one or two planes. They kept no premises, not even hangars, and did no maintenance themselves, beyond normal daily checks and perhaps 50-hour inspections. They got most of the major overhaul work and C of As done where ground maintenance facilities were established, and quite often in our workshops.

During 1955 we dropped over 1,200 tons of carrots for the rabbit boards, as well as vast amounts of supplies for the Forestry. The Dominies were proving invaluable for freighting as well as for the scenic work, and they could carry 1,200 lb of whitebait, which made freighting out from Big Bay much easier and quicker. They were too big for use at Martins Bay, but often we did a shuttle service ferrying 'bait out of Martins Bay with the Auster and transferring it to the Dominie at Big Bay. The Proctors had become an embarrassment, but we used them whenever possible for scenic and charter flying, and freighting 'bait out of Big Bay.

The Proctor V was useful for ambulance work, having been modified to carry a stretcher. In late 1955 we were at last granted a licence to operate it as an ambulance plane, and from then on it made many ambulance and funeral trips to all parts of New Zealand. Not long after, the Vincent Hospital Board gave permission for the Dunstan and Cromwell hospitals to use our service for the transportation of some of their patients, and so one more milestone was passed.

The Austers however, useful as they were, were gradually being superseded by more modern aircraft. We began to replace them with Cessna 180s. We had built two new blister hangars to house our growing fleet, and had now increased the Queenstown–Dunedin–Queenstown service to a daily one. Including John Kilian and myself there were now six pilots. Tex Smith joined the firm in 1951, and soon after a friend of his, Russell Troon, came too. Both had been topdressing for Bill Hewett at Mossburn and Russell had celebrated his appearance with a forced landing on the Frankton Flat. Trevor Cheetham was still with us, and we had Bruce Irving as a cadet pilot. I couldn't have wished for a better team: they flew long hours, and worked loyally for the firm. We had a great team on the ground staff too; two local boys were apprentice engineers, the late David Bell from Queenstown, and Alec Johnston of Lower Shotover.

With the Dominies proving so much cheaper to run, we decided to try to sell the Anson Mk XII. There was no market for the Mk I, but the Mk XII could be a useful proposition in the right place. It was in perfect condition, and still had no more than 650 hours up since new. Unfortunately Civil Aviation had just brought in new regulations regarding wooden-framed aircraft in tropical countries, so a good potential market was closed to us. It was decided at a directors' meeting that I should go to Australia on company business and at the same time try to sell the Anson. I flew to Christchurch to connect with the DC6 which was scheduled to leave that Friday night, but the weather was so bad that the Sydney–Christchurch plane had to turn back, and our flight was cancelled. The DC6 crew and I were staying at the same hotel, and over a couple of nightcaps we talked shop. We were discussing all aspects of flying, and they were asking me questions about aerial topdressing, and bush-flying activities.

The "hostie" was there too, apparently taking an intelligent interest in all the shop-talk. During a lull in the conversation she said, "Are you flying with us in the morning?"

"Oh, yes. That's why I'm having all these whiskies. I'm *so* nervous, I've never been up before."

She didn't bat an eyelid, so obviously she hadn't been listening to a word we'd been saying. I decided to lay it on. "It's this flying over water I don't like. It's a *terrible* thought."

"Oh, you'll be all right," she said. "I'll sit beside you while we take off."

"Will you hold my hand too?"

Yes, she would do that too. Soon after, we all retired, ready for an early start on the following day.

Six next morning was reporting time at the Christchurch Airport, and soon I was aboard the DC6 settling into a big roomy seat all to myself. The aircraft taxied out to the end of the runway and I leaned back quite relaxed, watching for loose rivets and oil leaks. While the engines were running up, I felt the seat sag beside me, and the half-forgotten conversation of the night before suddenly came back to me. Trying to look scared, I silently put my hand in hers.

As the aircraft gathered speed down the runway, I clung tighter and tighter, until when it climbed off she rose to leave, saying, "Do you think you'll be all right now?"

"Oh, I don't know. I could stand a lot of this."

"Well you mustn't be selfish. I have other passengers to attend to besides you."

"I'll try to be brave. I'll do my best," I quavered. At about 20,000 ft we levelled off, and as we were passing over the West Coast, she came back to my seat.

"A message for you, sir. The captain would like to see you on the flight deck."

"Will it be all right for me to walk?"

She replied somewhat tartly. "I'm walking, aren't I?"

"But you're different."

"Of course it's all right, just go ahead."

Making a show of being nervous I staggered up the aisle, reached the bulkhead door, passed through, and shut it. The skipper looked round, stepped out of his seat and indicated that I step in. He sat down in a spare crew seat, pulled his cap over his eyes, and settled back for a little bit of exaggerated rest, and I carried on driving. After some time the hostess came forward with the morning tea, and when she saw me sitting at the controls, and the skipper apparently asleep, she was definitely not amused.

Not long after, when I had returned to my seat, she came along with a drink, on a tray, and said freezingly, "Captain's compliments, after your *arduous* flight."

I apologised profusely, and endeavoured to smooth her ruffled feelings. I knew she was getting married soon, and I offered to make it up to her when she came to Queenstown for her honeymoon. But she wouldn't be cajoled: "I wouldn't trust you as far as I could see you!"

But I took her to dinner when we reached Sydney and a truce was made. She and her husband called on us when they came to Queenstown, and I took them home to meet my wife and spend an evening with us.

Guests at home were frequent, and one interesting visitor was the English cartoonist Chris Wren, well known for his "oddentifications" during the war (cartoons of aircraft types) and for his contributions and sketches in well-known aviation and other magazines. Chris was making a study of the aerial work being done in New Zealand and accompanied us on some topdressing and seed-sowing jobs. He acted as chucker-out for a supply-drop at the Fox Glacier, and was generally given a fair insight into the bush-flying side of New Zealand aviation.

Round about this time I had another forced landing. I was dropping some fencing material at Mt Torlesse in Canterbury, and had just climbed high enough to make the drop when there was a loud clattering, which later I found to be a broken con-rod that had gone through the crankcase. I jettisoned my load, switched off the motor, and glided down to land in a flat paddock at the foot of a homestead garden. A girl was so busy cutting a lawn with a motor mower that she neither saw nor heard me. I hadn't realised this, and was hardly prepared for the fright she got when she looked up and found me leaning over the fence watching her. She forgave me the scare I had given her, and pressed on me the usual country hospitality so universal in New Zealand.

An out-of-routine job came up when the Internal Affairs Department asked us to liberate some trout fry by air. This was to be the first time it had been done by air in the South Island, although I believe there had been an aerial liberation in the North Island the season before. On the morning of the drop the fry came in by road transport to the Frankton aerodrome. As we were using an aircraft which was normally engaged on rabbit-poisoning, no risk was taken of the fry becoming contaminated. They were packed into a canvas container before being placed in the hopper of the Cessna. The Internal Affairs Fisheries Officer, Chris Ulberg, used a tranquilliser drug to settle the fry, and to help place what was estimated to be 120,000 of them in the container.

After 50 minutes flying Tex Smith, who was piloting, was over the dropping site, Lake Paringa, about 44 miles south of the Fox Glacier. With improved accommodation and access this part of the world had become a popular fishing spot, and the Department had decided to improve the fishing by the liberation of rainbow trout. Brown-trout fishing was already very good and the addition of rainbow would increase the appeal to fishermen.

The drop was made from about 100 ft. Internal Affairs Officers waited below in boats, ready to observe the results, on a 24-hour survey, to determine whether the fry had suffered any ill effects. According to Departmental statistics, the survival rate of the annual hatch was not very large. It was estimated that out of every 250,000 hatched only 2,000 would survive, and out of this number about 1,700 would die of natural causes. So with these figures, not many were left for the angler. This was the reason why the fry were released in such large numbers, and the policy was to repeat the process in the succeeding years.

With our decision to go ahead and buy out the South West-land section of NAC, I formed a subsidiary company and called it West Coast Airways Ltd. We planned to fly a scheduled passenger service with freight and Post Office mail contracts between Hokitika and Haast; and we would run air taxi services, also carrying mail and freight, between Hokitika, Waiho, Whataroa, Milford Sound, and Greymouth. There would be joyriding from Hokitika and Greymouth to all air-fields south of Hokitika on the West Coast, and we would also do non-scheduled passenger and charter work, and short excursion flights. The four-times-weekly service run by NAC would be replaced with a daily schedule between Hokitika and Haast, a direct service without stops at Franz Josef or Fox Glacier. We would service the two glaciers on a separate schedule.

We did not intend to increase the fares, and hoped eventually to extend the service from Hokitika-Haast through to Milford. This would then connect with the Milford–Queenstown link run by the parent company, and so through to Dunedin on the Queenstown–Dunedin run. I thought this would make a valuable round trip right through from Hokitika to Dunedin. The connecting service with the Dakota run by NAC from Wellington to Hokitika would make it possible for overseas visitors to get right down the West Coast side of the South Island to Milford, and across to Dunedin, or down to Invercargill, in very quick time. For visitors with limited time this was one way to ensure that they would cover plenty of country, and it would give more and more people the chance to see something of what the South Island had to offer.

I applied for topdressing licences, and started giving demonstrations on various farm properties in an endeavour to interest West Coast farmers in the new medium. It was a calculated risk, but I felt we had an advantage over the nationally-run airline, because of our lower overheads and smaller staff. We were prepared to look for work outside the scheduled services, and in every way our mode of operation would be vastly more flexible.

The Queenstown–Dunedin service was in a category similar to that of the scheduled service to be operated from Hokitika to Haast. It had long been a losing proposition, and only now looked as if it might break even; but it produced intangible benefits: it rounded off our activities, gave us control of our area provided a vital service to the community, and put us on the map for incoming visitors. Some of the losses for the year could fairly have been considered advertising because of the goodwill generated and the indirect advertising we received, of which we were much in need, having no advertising formally budgeted in our annual estimates. I felt the good it did outweighed the loss. Having struggled so hard to get it going and having persevered when the loadings were low, I felt it was worth while hanging on now, as the tourist influx was increasing annually and in a few more years there would be a far greater volume of traffic. If it did nothing else it kept the aircraft fully utilised, which was most important. Although it was nothing to do with me in late 1960, I was sorry to see it then discontinued.

The Hokitika-Haast section, too, might well be for a time an expensive luxury, having to be supplemented by more paying sections of the business, but in time it would pick up and play its part.

I canvassed the area and had considerable work promised from the Lands and Survey Department for topdressing and lime-sowing in areas being farmed for resettlement. A certain amount of supply-dropping was promised from the Forest Service, together with supply-drops for private parties of stalkers or prospectors.

The late Tom Harris, who was then employed by NAC at Hokitika, was to stay on as a working partner in the new company. He was terrifically keen, energetic and enthusiastic, and was already spending his weekends canvassing farmers for aerial topdressing orders.

NAC were as helpful as possible over the transfer, and at last I was able to get a belated State Advances Rehabilitation loan. A very good friend in Wellington, through the help of an excellent lawyer and accountant, was able to impress the State Advances Corporation enough to have them approve the standard Rehab loan. More than that, I managed to procure one for both Kilian and Topliss who, also being returned servicemen, were eligible. These three loans, together with Tom Harris's share, provided some of the cash to buy the section from NAC together with the Dominies they had been operating there, and the office and hangar facilities at Hokitika.

Some of the existing office staff had agreed to stay on after the changeover, and with Tom Harris as resident engineer we were ready to get started. It was after all these weeks of work and organising that my partners in Queenstown went cold on the idea, and wanted to wash it up. This was an awkward situation, as during all the preliminaries they had appeared to be completely with me. I felt we couldn't go back on our agreement with NAC; besides, I had already finalised finance arrangements on my partners' behalf, as well as my own. Furthermore, I had so successfully demonstrated the potential of the proposed new airline that a syndicate of businessmen was anxious to take over if we did decide to pull out.

This would only have made way for a competitor to cash in on my weeks of promotion and forward bookings – as had happened in 1949, when my canvassing efforts and other promotion for topdressing was pressing along until at the final moment my partners went cold on the idea. This time, however, they agreed, grudgingly, to go ahead.

By this time other operators were pressing to be allowed to use the Milford strip. Until this time it was still a restricted airfield

The station 'bus only just fits astride the *Earnslaw*

A moment of relaxation: Popeye and Lorie in their home

Queenstown with Cecil Peak to the left

Milford Airstrip taken from above Cleddau River, looking down Milford Sound to the Tasman Sea

with only approved pilots of Southern Scenic Airservices Ltd licensed to land there. National Airways were keen to land the West Coast Dominies at Milford, and so the time had come for us to relinquish our rights and turn it over to the Government for extension. It would be too costly for us to do this ourselves, so by July 1956 the extensions had been completed, and four months before we took over the South Westland service, NAC made their inaugural flight celebrating the transition of the strip to a public airfield, licensed for Dominies. It was a red-letter day for us too, as now we could land our own Dominies there.

By November 1956 we had finalised the changeover, and started in business as West Coast Airways Ltd. Tom Harris, Barry Topliss, John Kilian, and myself were partners and equal shareholders. Tom was to be resident engineer, and we employed Brian McCook, a New Zealander who had been flying for Fiji Airways, as our first manager-pilot.

Tom Harris was about 36, married, with one daughter. He had long been associated with aviation on the West Coast, first as an aircraft engineer with Bert Mercer, and later, when Air Travel Ltd sold out to NAC in 1947, he stayed on in the employ of the Corporation. A private pilot also, he had a part-share in an aeroplane which he used for private flying jaunts on the weekend with his co-owners. Full of enthusiasm, very loyal, and a very hard worker, he was completely wrapped up in the company, and had great hopes for its future development. It was partly because of this that he lost his life just 11 months later.

On his last weekend alive he had been doing some private flying about the district, and was taking the opportunity to survey landing strips that would be suitable for aerial topdressing. Somehow on one of these surveys his aircraft went out of control; he crashed near Maruia Springs and was killed instantly. We were all shocked, none more so than myself. Tom had been well known and well liked.

Despite this tragedy the company gradually built up and grew in stature, carrying on the role of its parent company in all avenues of aviation: supply-dropping, charter, scenic and

L

freight work, joyriding, scheduled services, topdressing and other agricultural work, and mercy and ambulance flights, and all the diverse jobs that crop up for small bush-flying airlines.

After Brian McCook left, Mervyn Rumsay became manager. Among the foundation pilots were Ken Eden, Jack Humphries, and Paul Legg.

16

Grounded

BEING AWAY FROM HOME so much was beginning to
affect my domestic life. Since 1947 I had constantly been
absent for long periods, mostly supply-dropping, particularly when we were doing so much for the Forest Service
in the North Island. This kept me busy for weeks on end.
Often I was delayed by weather, and at times I hardly saw
the children. They'd be still in bed when I left in the morning,
during the rare times I was at home, and again in bed when
I got in at night, especially when I had been "out with the
boys".

The special occasions – birthdays, show-days, picnics and
anniversaries, even when one of my sons was born – were always
getting fouled up. Either I got home too late, or not at all, when
weather delayed me, usually on the West Coast and often up
north at Ruatahuna or in the Urewera country somewhere. No
wonder Lorie was getting fed up.

There was a lack of ready cash too. We were always hoping
for better times, but everything was swallowed up in the interests
of the firm. We were always promising ourselves a decent
living wage, and perhaps someday even a bonus, but it never
happened. It was always "maybe next year". The long-awaited
dividend never came while I was with the company. We paid
the best wages we could to our staff, and the pilots received such
fringe benefits as an extra $2 per hour on every revenue-pro-
ducing hour they flew. If they did 80 hours in a month, that was
an extra $160 on their basic wage. But this didn't apply to the
partners.

As the children got older and more and more was needed to

feed and clothe them Lorie turned to other means to augment the housekeeping. We had a large house and she started taking bed-and-breakfast guests during the peak of the tourist season when beds were at a premium. As I was away from home so much she had always attended to the household accounts, and I didn't fully realise how difficult she was finding it to manage. When I suggested that she had enough to do looking after five children without taking guests, she pointed out that we couldn't manage on the small salary we were paying ourselves, and particularly the extra strain that entertaining for the firm caused to the budget.

She had always been co-operative and helpful in this, and the goodwill it engendered brought a great deal of work to the firm, but my partners were always adamantly against an entertainment allowance of any kind being made, and equally adamant that their own wives should not be put to the extra work and expense of entertaining.

One night when I returned home unexpectedly after having been away for several weeks supply-dropping up north, I found the lounge cluttered with women's dresses in various stages of completion. I was staggered at the volume. I never questioned Lorie's judgement – if she needed a new dress she made arrangements to get it, usually doing her own dressmaking, but I couldn't see the need for all these. The mystery was solved when she admitted that she was making them up for a local dress-shop, working over a sewing-machine until the early hours while the children were safely in bed and she could work without interruption.

About this time Tom Donaldson, who had been our business manager for some time, decided to return to his old job, and so we tried to get someone to fill his place. In the meantime the bookwork began to get behind. It was a demanding job, with plenty to do, books to be kept, wages and accounts to do, bookings, statistics, and mail to attend to. The radio-telephone work was particularly exacting as we kept a continual listening watch, and the constant background of static and noise and the interruptions to take weather reports and reservations made working with figures a strain.

I went away on yet another supply-drop and as I was nearing home, I was surprised to hear over the intercom a voice remarkably like my wife's receiving weather reports and radioing flight plans. When I arrived at the aerodrome, I found her temporarily installed as business manager until such time as we could get a replacement.

Conditions in the office had become chaotic while I was away. Only the wages and bookings were up to date. One of my partners had asked Lorie if she would take over and straighten up for a few weeks, and she'd been only too pleased to help in any way she could. I was more than a little dubious about the arrangement, as I felt she'd quite enough to do, but she assured me she could manage.

This job stretched out to over two years. Apart from the boost to the budget, Lorie said she found it much easier to put up with my frequent absences from home, and she had less time to worry.

This was a year of much time away from home. We were all flat-out on aerial poisoning work and supply-dropping, then whitebaiting. There was the daily Dunedin schedule, and much scenic work. I had to be often on the Coast and at Hokitika attending licensing hearings, and forming the subsidiary and getting it going.

Trevor did some aerial spraying of sandflies at Milford Sound, around the Hotel area. Then we started a daily service to Invercargill. From NAC we had bought a fourth Dominie, ZK-AHS, which had once been used on the Dunedin–Invercargill route and piloted by the well known and popular Freddie Ladd before he left for a stint with Fiji Airways, later to return to New Zealand and start up NZ Tourist Air Travel, based at Auckland. The Invercargill–Queenstown section proved to be a liability and after a few months we abandoned it. There just wasn't enough patronage to keep it going.

An American Cinerama camera crew were in New Zealand

shooting part of a film to be called *Cinerama South Seas*. The publicity boost New Zealand would get, touristwise, would be of tremendous value, and so the late Johnny Hutchinson, a cameraman for the New Zealand National Film Unit, and liaison officer attached to the party, was most concerned when it appeared that the Milford Sound and Southern Lakes section might have to be missed out of the film because of lack of accommodation for the crew. There were two parties of about 16 technicians each, and while one covered the north the other was to come south. Weather delayed their schedule, and when they were due to come to Queenstown there was no accommodation available. Johnny was most disappointed about this, as in his opinion the Queenstown and Milford part was a must, and he didn't think the South could afford to lose such valuable publicity.

He rang us from Wellington to see if we could possibly find some accommodation. There was none to be had in the district and Lorie suggested that rather than have them by-pass the area, we should put them up in our own home, which was roomy enough. He was glad to accept the offer. Lorie was at that time employed full-time at the aerodrome, so could not cater for full meals for the party of 18 that eventually came, but she made up beds throughout the house and gave them supper every evening during their stay. The rest of their meals they arranged to have out. The whole team rose about 4.30 each morning and drove in their chartered bus to Queenstown, where one of the hotels had undertaken to give them breakfast at 5, a midday meal when required, and dinner at night. They worked long hours and were pretty exhausted by suppertime, and went to bed early.

They were accompanied by a Sandringham flying-boat, chartered from Ansett and flown out to New Zealand by an all-Australian crew. This was used to take the high-level shots in the Mount Cook, Franz Josef, and Fox Glacier areas, and for the air-to-air shots of the Mount Cook Airways Auster flying in the confined space of Milford Sound. Most of the supporting flying with small aircraft was done by Harry Wigley's Mount Cook Airservices in their Auster, with the bulky and unwieldy camera and batteries strapped beneath each wing. Only one of our aircraft was used, to provide foreground shots against the Southern Alps.

In appreciation of her gesture in enabling them to film the Milford area, which they considered magnificent, the producer, Richard Goldstein, invited my wife to fly with them while they filmed the Mt Cook section. She had to be up very early to accompany them down to the flying-boat anchored at Kelvin Grove on the Frankton Arm of Lake Wakatipu. Considerable time had to be spent assembling the camera in the flying-boat, and much patience needed, especially when a very special and valuable lens came loose and fell into the lake. Much valuable time was lost while a chartered launch located and salvaged the lens, and all the time anxious eyes were scanning the skies for changes in the weather.

The film was estimated to cost $ U.S. two million and was intended to show for one hour, featuring New Zealand and Australia. The 10 days of flying and ground shots of the South Westland area must have cost a fortune, but in the film they accounted for barely half a minute.

I had an interesting and rather exacting job contour-flying around the Buller Gorge area, with a scintillometer, a very sensitive geiger counter, installed in the Auster. This was soon after Messrs Cassin and Jacobsen made their uranium strike in the Buller Gorge. Mr T. J. McKee, managing director of the Nelson Lime and Marble Co., engaged me to prospect the area by air with the scintillometer. The company had staked claims over nearly 5,000 acres, and newspaper reports gave glowing predictions of uranium reserves estimated at between 20 and 40 dollars. I was accompanied by a geophysicist who took readings as we flew around at treetop level in difficult and heavily bushed country but results were negative, as we found that the sensitivity of the scintillometer was screened by the dense bush. My passenger wasn't sorry to be relieved of the necessity of any more contour-flying, which he described as "terrifying".

The Nelson firm was associated with an Australian company, the Rio Australian Proprietary Ltd, a subsidiary of Rio Tinto, one of the biggest mining organisations in the world. The New Zealand company had pegged out claims nearly a year before, and had been working for about eight months prospecting in very rough terrain. At that time they had located at least six uranium seams on the northern side of the Gorge just opposite where the original strike was made by Cassin and Jacobsen. In the U.S.A. ore containing 0·1 per cent or 0·2 per cent was considered commercial grade, but the Buller Gorge ore was, according to newspaper reports, assaying out at 1 per cent, 2 per cent, even as high as 5 per cent; but the main concern was whether it was present in payable quantities.

Camps were being established for working parties, and I airfreighted in some supplies, but most of the stuff was being flown in by helicopter.

In between prospecting by air and getting enthusiastic about uranium we were developing better ways to drop fencing material by air. In February we began laying a five-mile fence in Central Otago. Two of our Cessnas piloted by Tex and Russell dropped all the materials in under 6½ hours for Messrs H. and J. Stokes of Ardgour. Fifty bundles of wire were dropped, and a later inspection showed that 85 per cent landed right on target, undamaged. We dropped 2,100 standards, 50 H-iron posts, and 168 coils of No 8 wire altogether. Any damage sustained was only minor. The estimated time to complete a job such as this in the old way, was 15 to 20 days. This was the first drop to be done under the control and supervision of government departments, and the success of the operation set the seal of approval.

Hard on this drop came another for the Barker brothers of Ben Lomond Station, Queenstown, for three miles of fencing. At no time did the fencers have to move more than a few yards

to collect their material, and in three weeks the fence was completely erected. Only two iron standards were bent, and no
material was lost or wasted.

This was a year of extremes. We had one of the driest summers
for years. Summer at Frankton was always a time of fire-risk
during a dry season, but this summer was particularly bad. The
tinder-dry grass and plantations of gums and pines at various
places presented a real hazard. The nearest firefighting equipment was at Queenstown, five miles away, and so once a home
or one of the unoccupied cottages was threatened there wasn't
much hope of saving it. One season we put out 16 fires in a
couple of weeks in our little built-up area.

One of the biggest fire hazards was a belt of bone-dry pine
trees sheltering the arodrome. A fire here would threaten the
hangar installations, the aeroplanes parked outside, and the
hospital near by, so we kept the topdressing loader truck at the
ready, with 44-gallon drums set up on the tray, filled with water,
and with a pile of coalsacks soaking and ready for firefighting.

Later in the year, in direct contrast, there was severe local
flooding, and the lake rose 10 ft above normal. Water was knee-
deep outside the Mount Cook Company office, and the cellars of
Eichardts Hotel were flooded; one of the shopkeepers in Rees
Street had to evacuate his home and shop, and the two wharves
on the waterfront were awash. The esplanade wall was pounded
by such heavy waves that some of it broke away, and the
steamer *Earnslaw*, at the height of a gale, had to retire to the
Frankton Arm for shelter, riding the storm out with the help of
a 2-ton block anchor until the morning.

There were slips through the Kawarau Gorge, and on the
Kingston–Lumsden highway, cutting off the town from fresh
supplies. When groceries and fresh vegetables ran short we had
to run a ferry service, flying in fresh supplies for the hotels. That
February 70 in. of rain were recorded at Milford Sound, and
when I flew the Australian manager for Trans-Canada Airlines
into Milford, I found part of the airstrip washed away by
the flood waters. His experience of landing fields for Super

Constellations inspired him to comment that from the air our modest little strip "looked like a sheep-track".

By the middle of 1958 my wife was still employed as business manager at the aerodrome. My partners were negotiating for somebody suitable to take her place, as she was hoping to be able to give up the job.

For some years we had been flying hunting and fishing parties into South Westland, Fiordland, and elsewhere, and were constantly aware of the limitations of a land-based plane. We fancied a Nordyn Norseman floatplane, used in Canada for this sort of work and capable of carrying a ton of freight or 10 to 12 passengers; but finance wasn't available and as an alternative we were considering putting floats on the Cessna – this was done after 1960. We discussed the prospect of building hunting lodges in suitable places, particularly at Martins Bay, but the uncertainty of getting accommodation at Queenstown if weather delayed us getting in was always a problem. As it was, Lorie sometimes made accommodation available for stranded clients in our home, but only as an emergency measure.

Now that she had decided to leave the office she was toying with the idea of taking over a little country hotel a mile away from the aerodrome. Apart from anything else, she thought this might help us in guaranteeing accommodation for the firm's clients. She was now used to the routine of being a working wife, and had found that it had what she called a "therapeutic value". She'd decided to go on working because during that year she'd kept a diary, and had found that in the whole year I had only been at home for 10 weeks, and that even during these weeks my longest unbroken stay before going off on another job for the firm had been four days. (During this year the subsidiary at Hokitika had necessitated more time away than usual.) She told me that if the firm was going to go on demanding so much of my time, a busy life and another interest for her were essential if we were to preserve the family unity.

She asked me if I would agree to her buying the hotel and

whether I'd have any objection to our shifting down there to live. She would run it, and it would keep her busy and independent. It could be run without disruption to my own work, or any neglect to the family, and in fact it was the only way she could carry on working and still look after the family properly.

I was all in favour, for I realised that if we had some normal routine home life with freedom from financial stress there would be no need for her to take on office work for "therapy".

So in May 1958 we bought the Lower Shotover Hotel, just past the Lower Shotover Bridge, and made plans to move in. Neither of us had had any experience whatever in running a hotel, nor did we understand the responsibilities involved in being publicans, and we had no clues on what we were letting ourselves in for.

We didn't discuss our plans with my partners, apart from Lorie giving in her notice. A week before she was due to leave the aerodrome one of my partners tackled us about the proposed shift to the hotel. He was quite put out; he thought that a "pub" would "reflect on the firm".

This brought out into the open what had been a gradual decline in my good relationships with my partners. Having been away so much I hadn't really been aware of it, and all this came as a bit of a shock. But life went on in much the same way in the flying business and the hotel began to pick up trade. We made alterations and improvements, and my wife held the licence and managed the hotel.

I helped after work at night whenever I was home, and my partners considered this was disloyalty to the firm, although they didn't tell me this until some months later. By 1959 I at last realised that the *esprit-de-corps* of the company was gone, and there was no future there for my sons or myself; I began to consider the possibility of getting back to the land.

My daughter had started nursing, and my four sons were growing up sturdy and loved country life. I began to make tentative inquiries about back-country places; in the first place because that type of country appealed to me, and in the second place we wanted to find somewhere with plenty of potential for development, and not over-capitalised. Price of course was a major consideration. I could expect a certain amount from my shares in the company, and in fact had been offered a very generous price from an overseas investor with whom one of my partners had been in touch some weeks before.

Eventually I had signed up to buy Cecil Peak Station, on Lake Wakatipu, and had offered my shares to my partners according to the articles of association of the company, intending also put them in the picture regarding the overseas investor who was prepared to supply any amount of much-needed capital without many strings attached, and to leave the management of the company and the majority of shares in the hands of the remaining partners.

I didn't get a chance to discuss this. One afternoon while I was in Queenstown arranging a large bank overdraft for the company, and supplying my own personal guarantee on practically everything I owned, plus a substantial guarantee by my father, my partners voted me out of the firm. When I returned to the aerodrome after successfully negotiating the overdraft I found a letter addressed to me on the notice board. The letter informed me that my services were no longer required, and that employment would cease forthwith. The reason given was that I was not giving my whole time and attention to the firm. I felt that my logbook and record of hours flown in the service of the company disproved this.

This was on the evening of 22 December 1960 and, as can be imagined, it was not a very happy Christmas for our family, for I was now without a livelihood.

There was now a grave crisis in our lives. I had paid a substantial deposit on Cecil Peak, confident that the financial requirements could be met. We hoped to sell the hotel, but the trade was so depressed at that time that half the hotels in Central Otago and Southland seemed to be on the market. It was the wrong time to hope for a speedy sale; in fact we couldn't sell and it had to be leased for six years as the only alternative.

My shares in the company were worthless now, as nobody could afford to take the risk of buying them without a controlling interest. I had to settle up for the station in four months, or lose it and my deposit, and I was bound to recover my father's money, as he had shares in the company too.

The next four months were ones I would not like to go through again. It took a terrific lot of readjustment. After flying constantly for the last 12 years, thinking, eating and sleeping aviation, being so completely wrapped up in the firm, with everything orientated to its needs, it was like losing an arm or an eye to be so suddenly catapulted out of it.

True, I had been going to retire to farming, but I had planned for a more gradual transition. For the last 12 years there had hardly been a day when I had not been at the aerodrome or on company business somewhere, either at daylight or by 8 a.m. as, indeed, were most of the pilots, particularly when seasonal work demanded early starts to topdress, rabbit-poison, or catch early tides.

Although I had been in agreement with my wife over her buying the hotel, I had never visualised making it my livelihood; in fact the idea appalled me. Although the hotel had always been one of the favourite haunts of the pilots and myself after work was over, it was different living there. While I was still flying I didn't mind.

When we first moved in the year before, my wife had said, "After the firm, the Shotover pub has always been your second home. You like it so much, that I bought it for you."

Poetic justice! Then it was a joke; but now, still in perfect health and with years of flying ahead of me, I was dismayed. However much I now felt like an eagle caged, I could only be grateful for my wife's foresight in having taken on a business that gave us a roof over our heads. She'd seen all this coming long before I had.

Whatever else it did, it made me realise just how much I owed to my family, and how much I'd been neglecting them, not deliberately, but because I'd never realised that the firm had become something of an obsession over all those years, gobbling up all outside interests. This devastating experience drew the family together as nothing else could.

There were rumours that I had had to leave the firm because I could not pass the yearly medical examination required to retain my commercial licence, but this was untrue, as I was still fit, and passing my medicals with flying colours. In fact, I only relinquished my commercial licence in 1965 as, having turned 50, I now had to have the medicals every six months. This required too much time away from home, and it was also difficult to keep my flying hours up, although over the years since 1960, Bill Hewett has often, and very generously, pressed me to make use of one of his aircraft.

So ended my flying career.

17

New Horizons

I T WAS NOW April 1960, time to take possession of Cecil
Peak. During all the years of flying in this district I had
many times looked down appreciatively on this station,
situated in a beautiful, hidden valley surrounded by many old
English trees. It is guarded to the north by the jumbled tops of
Cecil Peak, marked on the map as being 6,477 ft but showing on
an aircraft altimeter as being over 6,700 ft. To the south the
serrated profile of Bayonet Peaks, 5,500 ft, effectively shelters
and dominates the cluster of station buildings at its foot. The
eastern boundary includes 20 miles of shore, lapped by the blue
waters of Lake Wakatipu. To the west are 18 miles of a superb
fly-fishing river, the Lochy. North-west from here, the Killie-
crankie Creek saddles into McKinlay's Creek, and finds its outlet at the far north-west of the property, Table Bay, adding to
the impression that Cecil Peak Station is an island, when in fact
it is no such thing, being merely part of the land mass on the
west side of Wakatipu that stretches back towards Mossburn and
the northern end of the Southland Province.

I used to think what a wonderful spot it could be, never
imagining that some day we'd be living there. I had always
fancied owning a property across the lake since visiting Walter
Peak Station in 1946; at that time I had been inspecting a
property called Closeburn, just opposite, in the Moke Lake
area, with the intention of buying it, but had eventually decided
in favour of going back into flying. In 1959 Walter Peak
Station, owned by the Mackenzie family since 1881, came on the
market, and this crystallised my decision to retire from commercial aviation. The property was auctioned, but I could see no

way of finding sufficient finance to buy and develop it. Then out
of the blue, I found myself making a down payment on the
neighbouring station, Cecil Peak.

Although I had no experience of high-country farming, I felt
I could learn. I was a farmer's son, had grown up on a farm,
albeit a low-country one, and could count on plenty of valuable
advice from my father and my four farming brothers. For the
past 14 years, I had been associated indirectly but intimately
with high-country farming through the experiments with
rabbit-poisoning, and seed-sowing, and the evolving of air-drop
fencing. I felt I had some knowledge of the risks involved in farm
management, and that what I didn't know I could learn,
though probably the hard way, by my own mistakes.

I knew there were indeed risks. Wool prices were down,
freight charges were high, labour costs rising all the time, and
labour, even then, difficult to obtain. High-country farming
could be called the Cinderella of New Zealand agriculture and
there were plenty of people who did not hesitate to say so, including those engaged in it. On Cecil Peak, wool-growing was
the only real source of revenue; there was no scope for diversify-
ing with crops, as the lake effectively prevented the hiring of
contractors to harvest them, and it wasn't economic to buy
costly headers and other equipment. Lambing percentages were
not high, and when we took over there were only about 80 head
of cattle on the place.

Nevertheless Lorie and I saw great potential, and we knew
that this was the life for us, whatever the hardships and risks
ahead. I could see no real future in growing wool only; all the
signs pointed to a trend that had steadily become more obvious
over the succeeding eight years, brought about by greater competition from synthetics, rising costs and wage rates, a shortage of
skilled labour, and a steady decline in wool prices. Apart from
the growing of wool I could see a tourist potential and scope for
increasing the cattle-carrying capacity of the property. This
would give us some of the necessary diversification, so that if the
wool market did decline we would have some other source of

income to fall back upon. However, to start with I hoped to improve the quality of the wool, and the weight, and the lambing percentages, and with a fencing and topdressing programme to raise the stock-carrying capacity.

The official date for the takeover was 1 April 1960, but we did not move into the Station until 12 days later. We had leased the hotel, and after the changeover the night before, had driven into Queenstown to stay at Eichardts Hotel. Our rooms overlooked Queenstown Bay, and directly opposite, rising above the sparkling waters of the lake, was Cecil Peak, already snow-capped, and with the lower slopes blackened by a recent burn.

At dawn the next morning we were busy taking the last of our possessions down to the Railway Wharf, to be put aboard the veteran lake steamer *Earnslaw*, which was getting up steam before making her twice-weekly trip down to Kingston. We cast off, and half an hour later were tying up alongside the Cecil Peak wharf, where once again all our belongings had to be off-loaded, either manually or with the help of a crane. The next two days were mostly occupied with getting our gear the one and a half miles up the valley to the homestead.

The takeover muster was not yet over, and the homestead swarmed with people – our own family, and a team of musterers. By the end of April, however, things had settled down a little. With no school nearer than Queenstown, Lorie had to start teaching the family with the help of the Correspondence School. She had written away some time before to enrol the three younger boys, and in a few days the first sets of school lessons had arrived.

We settled down to an autonomous existence, completely dependent on ourselves for almost all the necessities of life.

There was plenty of work that year (and every year since, come to that) but the first year always seems the worst. I could see hundreds of things waiting to be done, the only trouble being the vast amount of money required to achieve any results.

M

The hay-paddocks needed resowing and topdressing. Miles of fencing were required to make new blocks or to replace or renew the existing fences. There were gates to be re-made or re-hung. The mechanical equipment was old and constantly in need of repair, and the general maintenance bills were enor-mous. The diesel plant which supplied us with 7·5 kW of 230 voltage was continually breaking down, and all too often we would have to revert to the use of candles or lamps.

That first year was a dead loss. The wages bill alone was more than half the gross income. Because I had not farmed high-country before, and because part of the country is leased from the Crown, the Land Department had the right to insist that I employ a head shepherd, approved by them, for the first three years. Actually, with the price of wool what it was, and the property being understocked, the number of men he deemed necessary to run the place proved an expensive luxury. The wool clip was only half what I expected. At the final count for take-over the original 7,200 sheep which were to go with the station had dwindled to 6,400; a large proportion of this flock needed culling, and in many the wool was "run out". Lambing percentages were low, and consequently we couldn't cull as thoroughly as we would have liked. That first season our returns worked out at $2·35 per head, but the costs to operate reached $2.40.

I have often heard people discuss the work done by the high-country farmer, comparing it with his low-country cousin. Mostly they seem to think that apart from the main musters of the year, and the shearing, the high-country man has nothing to do but sit around and wait for the wool to grow. This is a long way from the truth; true, we can plan our work more easily than say a dairyfarmer can, but the real fact is that there's never enough time to do all the things one can see wanting to be done.

The various musters came around relentlessly. Our first one is the fall or autumn muster. Normally this takes about a month. The wethers have to be brought in from the dark summer country away out at the back of the run, and eye-clipped and dipped, before being hunted out on to their winter blocks on the warm sunny faces. The ewes too are eye-clipped, crutched, dipped, and drenched, and the last season's lambs are weaned and inoculated and put through the same routine of drenching and dipping before also being pushed out on to their winter country. Then the ewes, having been kept in the paddocks to go to the ram in the first week in May, are, six weeks later, hunted out too.

By this time the early snows will have come, and with any luck a good snowcap will have built up on the tops. This is always a help, and saves much extra work, as the sheep, once brought down, will stay below the snowline. If the winter is mild, without much snow, one is constantly watching for a fall in the barometer, prepared, if bad weather is on the way, for a quick sortie up the mountain to bring down sheep which have wandered back up to the higher ground.

June and July are the slackest months of the year, but there are still plenty of chores to do. Morning and evening milkings of the house-cows, pups and weaner pigs to be fed with the surplus milk, dog-tucker sheep to be killed and skinned every few days, plus "muttons" to kill and dress out for meat for the house. There is the seven-days-a-week job of feeding-out hay or silage to the stock grazing in the valley – usually 50 or 60 rams, all the station horses, the five or six house-cows, and the cattle, plus the old sheep kept down for dog-tuckers. There are dogs and hens to feed, but the turkeys, ducks, and geese forage for themselves. When the ground is not too frozen, there's always fencing to be done, gates to be made and hung, drains and ditches to be cleared. Constant mechanical repairs are required to keep the two tractors, Land-Rover, other farm implements, and the two tourist buses in going order. Not to mention servicing water pumps, the diesel-lighting plants – one at the homestead, and one down at the shearers' quarters – and the shearing plant in the woolshed.

All too soon, preparations are under way again to start shearing. Men have to be contacted and booked up for the muster. The shearing gang is usually engaged from the season before. Apart from the general farm work which goes on, this time of the year means rising at any time from 1.30 a.m. on to cook early breakfast for the musterers, so that they can get out on the hill before daylight, and at times to take a beat oneself with the gang.

Before the shearing gang arrive there is the usual checking and cleaning out of their quarters and cookshop, getting the cookshop rationed if the gang requires it for the shearers' cook who comes with the gang, pumping water ready for their use, checking the water pump, the shearing plant, and the lighting plant for serviceability, and fervently hoping that this time there will be no last minute breakdowns. (This is always the time when previously reliable machinery chooses to pack up and parts are urgently needed for repairs, and this is when our lack of orthodox communications is most severely felt.)

We usually start shearing in the first week in September, amid some tension. Apart from wondering, up to the last moment, whether all the promised musterers will turn up, there's always the likelihood that the shearing gang will be held up by the weather or by late cutting-out from another station. This is the time when we find out how many sheep we have lost during the winter, either through old age, keas, wool-blindness, tetanus, falling over bluffs, or diseases due to mineral deficiencies in the soil.

After being shorn, the sheep are ear-tagged, then drenched for worms, inoculated against tetanus and black-leg, and put through the swim dip before being mustered out again on to their respective blocks. The ewes are shorn before lambing, but there are always a few early lambs baa-ing about, determined to get themselves mismothered. The rams are foot-rotted and drenched, then for a short while the sheep work eases up a little, except for "straggling" to bring in sheep missed on the main muster. From time to time small mobs of stragglers are brought in, shorn by ourselves, as the shearers have by now moved on to other stations. In December there is the tailing muster, when the new season's lambs are put through the ritual of being earmarked, docked and tailed.

In between the sheep work there is cattle mustering and cattle work to do, and much repairing of the fences that they have broken down. Some of the cattle on the station when we took over were a pretty mixed breed, and very wild. The really wild ones were all running out at the back of the property and, never having known fences, were brutes to muster. A fence in the line of flight meant nothing to them; they walked, ran, jumped or struggled through it. We wasted much time and made several expensive musters trying to get them out. As I wanted them all off the property as soon as possible, a team of six men, including myself, were out for days trying to round them up, and it required all our combined experience, patience, and temper, to do so. The cattle were suspicious and scary, constantly breaking back and stampeding all the rest. They would go anybody on foot or on horseback. When at last we did get any of them down to the home paddocks among the quieter cattle, they upset and disturbed them, broke down and wrecked fences, and headed off back where they came from, not stopping until they reached their old haunts some 20 miles back at the head of the Lochy River. They gave us some wild and hilarious times, and plenty of talk around the fire in the back huts at night, recounting individual experiences during the day.

When at last they were all in and corralled in the yards down at the wharf, the hardest job was yet to come – getting them aboard the steamer. The *Earnslaw* called in early, in anticipation of a delay in loading, and the next two or three hours were spent trying to get the stubborn brutes up the ramp into the pens on the upper deck. Once the lead animal had gone quietly up the ramp and stepped on deck, the chances were that the rest would follow without trouble, but time and again somebody on board would spook the lead animal at the crucial moment, perhaps when he was just about to set his ponderous weight on the deck. A deckhand would choose that moment to peer around a corner, or make a quick movement along the deck, and in a second the steer would turn and crash his way down the ramp and along the wharf, with the rest just as mindless, belting along after him.

Once, after almost a solid hour, we had just succeeded in getting one big brute with a wicked-looking spread of horn nicely up the ramp, and the rest following perfectly, when a crewman chose that moment to stroll past the top of the ramp, casually flicking something white over his shoulder as he went. The bullock broke back, and there was absolute pandemonium. Men scaled the wharf rails in all directions. The whole mob bolted back along the wharf, breaking down hurdles, and some, bursting clear out of the main barrier at the far end, took off for the back country and weren't recovered again for several weeks.

It was a long and frustrating three hours getting this particular mob out. Hours of effort and excitement and colourful language, and dark mutterings about clots with tea-towels. However, despite the unfamiliar sights and sounds of the steamer tied up at the wharf, with steam hissing, bells clanging, shouted orders, and noise from the engine-room, the cattle were at last safely on board, and steaming off to Kingston railhead, where they were offloaded into railway trucks and railed to the Lornevill or Burnside saleyards.

The few we couldn't get were eventually shot, as they were only a nuisance where they were, ruining fences and teaching our quieter cattle bad habits.

That first year at the Station I kept a Piper PA18 at the homestead on a reciprocal arrangement with the owner, who wanted somewhere in the area to keep it on standby for hiring out. I acted as a ferry pilot, ferrying it wherever it was to be used for hire, and in return I could have it for my own use, paying only for my own petrol and oil and maintenance checks, but being charged the usual hiring rate for any work I did for hire and reward. This suited me fine, and after shearing was finished I sowed 70 tons of super for Phil Hunt, owner of Mt

Nicholas Station. I did some sheep-spotting and hunting-down for myself during one particularly cold spell, when the snow lay thick everywhere. This gave rise to a story in an overseas magazine that I did my mustering from the air but, in fact, aerial mustering in this sort of country isn't satisfactory; it can be done better on foot with the dogs. However, using an aircraft, such as an Auster or Piper for hunting-down or snow-raking, when snow is imminent, can be very helpful.

The winter was a hard one: it rained and hailed and snowed. The roof leaked, waterpipes burst, lavatory bowls froze then cracked open, and finally the lighting plant, which had been continually breaking down, packed up completely, and the household once again had to resort to candles. In the middle of this I was in hospital in Dunedin for three weeks, having a hernia repair operation.

Lorie had her hands full teaching the boys and cooking for the family and the three to four shepherds we had on the payroll for most of the year. Everywhere one looked there was work to be done, made more tedious because of lack of capital to do more than go on patching up old and worn-out equipment. We dug and drained ditches, did the inevitable fencing and other repairs, graded and gravelled the short length of road to the homestead. We wasted hours with broken-down tractors and other machinery, and spent more wasted hours patching up the unpatchable. All the buildings needed a facelift, to be repainted, to have old guttering and leaking downpipes replaced, and the walls repaired where the overflowing water had rotted the timber.

There was an outbreak of distemper in the district, and all our dogs and those belonging to the shepherds had to be taken out to Lake Hayes, where the dogs from about the district were inoculated.

The main house needed much attention. The earlier owners had contemplated rebuilding, but we had to shelve any such idea. It was almost impossible to get tradesmen over to do the work – and anyway we couldn't afford it. Lorie could not bear to leave the interior the way it was, and embarked on a long and ambitious interior decorating scheme, in her "spare" time. (Very spare indeed.) After schooling and housekeeping were done for the day she would tackle the painting and papering of one or other of the many rooms. On several occasions, having gone early to bed, I would wake at some unearthly hour and go looking for her, to find her balanced on a ladder, painting a ceiling, a candle in one hand and a paintbrush in the other.

Then suddenly summer was with us. In January the heat was intense, and haymaking was a real chore, with temperatures soaring to well over 120 degrees in the open. The sun beat down on perspiring bodies; to dodge what heat we could, we would start haymaking just as soon as the dew was off the hay, and mow, ted, bale and cart in, until time for a late lunch about 2 p.m. Lunch over, with the heat so intense, we would often leave off until 4 o'clock when, although it was still very hot, the sun would be disappearing behind Cecil Peak. Somebody would bring up tea and sandwiches and cordials at about 6 p.m. and haymaking would continue until twilight, or alternatively until the evening dew became too heavy. Then home for a late dinner at about 10.

By December 1961 our daughter Wendy had married Neville Turner, whose father was an orchardist at Millers Flat near Roxburgh; Richard had completed his schooling at Waitaki Boys' High School; and David had withdrawn from Correspondence School and gone to Waitaki as a boarder. Our first head shepherd had moved on, and the next one had gone to work for a neighbour. After that we dispensed with any more head shepherds, and cut down on permanent manpower, relying on casual musterers for the main musters, and doing the rest of the work ourselves, with the help of our son-in-law who came up to work with us for a couple of years.

I got hold of some pheasants' eggs and tried to rear pheasants to release on the property as gamebirds. They were difficult to hatch, our broody hens getting unbroody at the wrong times.

Eventually we raised five, only to find that they were all cocks. However Bill Hewett, who had been breeding them quite successfully, gave us four hens, and so we released them in the valley. For some time they hung about the homestead, but gradually moved off into more secluded places. They are slowly increasing; often the shepherds see signs of them or some of the chicks but so far we have refrained from shooting them.

There is some social life when we can find time to enjoy it, or when our poor communications give us the opportunity to find out about an occasion before it is already over. With the steamer calling in only twice a week, our papers used to come in bundles, several days late. Telephone communication is so bad that people have given up trying to reach us by this means. Often telegrams, sent on by post, arrive days late, sometimes long after an intending guest has already been and gone.

We usually like to attend the agricultural shows at Lake Hayes and at Wanaka, but the family never take their horses to compete in the riding events because of the difficulty and time it takes to get them shipped out and to the showgrounds, especially Wanaka, which is over 80 miles away. Also they don't have the time to school them, or to get to any of the riding schools held at various times during the year, to give them polish and instruction. Nor, when they were younger, could they attend pony club meetings. Nevertheless their riding is adequate for the work they do about the station. For the last two seasons they have attended the annual sports day and gymkhana at Glenorchy, riding their horses up the west side of the lake, through the properties of Walter Peak, Mt Nicholas, Elfin Bay, and the Greenstone Stations, and fording the Dart River at Kinloch. If all has gone well, eventually, after about two days, they reach Glenorchy, somewhat scratched, tired, and many times soaked, having usually had to swim the horses round bluffs and bays, where the track is more often than not under water with a rise in lake levels after heavy rain in the back country.

N

Most of the small population of nearly 100 residents of Glenorchy attend the meeting, plus men from neighbouring stations, bringing their horses and competing in the programmed races. There are trophies and prizes and the day winds up with a dance at the local hall, where the trophies are presented.

The autumn usually merits a visit from the RNZAF to show the flag. After the displays there is a bit of socialising, and the Air Force would be sadly out of character if they didn't make the most of their time off duty. The Central Flying School's Harvard aerobatic team give a faultless display of formation aerobatics and smoke-trailing, and on other occasions when the RNZAF Sunderland has shown the flag their display of low-level flying over the little township, hemmed in by mountains, has been impressive.

I usually try to get over during the weekend to renew acquaintanceship. On one occasion the aerobatic team were accompanied by a Devon. They planned to return to Wigram on the day following their display, but were weatherbound until the following Tuesday.

During this weekend I found myself installed, quite un-officially, but with much pomp and ceremony, as Station Commander, RNZAF, Queenstown. The crews paraded up the main street of Queenstown, led by a Flight Lieutenant as drum major, twirling the hotel broom in accepted style, while in the midst several brawny airmen carried me bodily to the installation. Earlier we had all been very social in the house bar of the hotel where most of the crews were staying. At 11 the bar closed, and there'd been a general exodus of Air Force guests, including some bewildered American tourists, who found themselves caught up in the fun and games and spent a hilarious couple of hours taking part in the parade and the late supper turned on in the dormitory where the rest of the crew were billeted.

It had been raining for hours, and the next day we chartered the launch to go back to the Station to collect our sons, who had been minding the place and doing the milking. The Air Force came with us for the trip, smart in their best "blues". The Land-Rover had gone unserviceable, and there were loud cries of anguish when the tractor and trailer we were using instead splashed through a particularly deep rut and muddied all their pants. One immaculate Flight Lieutenant found himself down at the cow byre helping one of our boys finish the milking, and happily hosed down the yards, the cows, and the milkboy with cheerful impartiality and disregard for his own best "number one's" uniform. They wanted to see my airstrip, and when I showed it to them the Squadron Leader said, "You're joking, of course!"

The locals still talk of the night the Sunderland flying-boat was sold. During after-dinner conviviality, a Southland farmer heard some talk of the Sunderlands being withdrawn from the service, and with his eye somewhat blearily on the main chance bargained to buy the Sunderland, and eventually handed over a cheque for $50. He insisted on inspecting his "buy", but while stepping aboard from the launch he fell into the Lake, which somewhat dampened his enthusiasm. Next day the cheque was pinned up in a prominent place in the cocktail bar at Eichardts Hotel, but history doesn't relate whether the Air Force honoured the deal, or what the farmer intended to use his bargain for.

The Station passed its own centenary while we were too busy to do more than record it in the diary, but we did join in the Wakatipu celebrations when the district centenary was reached in 1962. On the first of August every willing male agreed to grow a genuine beard. They paid a deposit of $1, which was to be forefeited if they shaved before the Centenary was over. The grand finale came when the beard-judging contest was held after ten days of celebrations. Over 600 beards were judged, and to my own surprise I came fourth. The removal of our beards was somewhat nerve-racking: the stage was set up with a one-stand shearing plant. There were bets on the weight of the best beard after removal. Instruments for taking off the whiskers were many and various; and besides scissors and the conventional electric razors, there was a murderous collection of blade shears, razor-sharp axes, and hedge-clippers.

Air NZ and NAC had jointly sponsored my beard and a telegram had been sent congratulating "all the furry ones, from their feathered friends", and backing me to "win by a whisker".

18

Visitors and Telephones

SOME TIME IN 1961 we began to consider the tourist possibilities of the Station. Visitors were often keen to see a
high-country property, but we had little time to show them
around. We very much enjoyed meeting them and they seemed
to get great pleasure out of visiting the place but the more
people came the more it cut into our work, and the best thing
seemed to be to put these visits on to a business basis. In that
way station work could go on without interruption, and the
visitors could be given a much better idea of the place.

We had repainted and redecorated the cottages and shearers'
quarters, and now we furnished them and rented them to
families for the holidays. At the homestead, we set aside half the
house for guests to stay in on a daily tariff. They hunted, fished,
rode horses, climbed, tramped, painted landscapes, or recovered
from illnesses or heart attacks, sometimes having been sent to us
by their doctors. Often they come just to relax and to get away
from what they term the rat-race.

At the same time we were ready to start a daily tourist trip
from Queenstown to the Station. Having secured the promise of
co-operation with one of the tourist launch operators, Mr Ray
Tomkies, master of the launches *Moana* and *Muritai II*, we
applied for a continuous passenger service licence to operate a
bus from our wharf up to the homestead, and with the acquisition of both the licence and a bus, we were ready to start. However, when we were ready to ship the bus over on the steamer,
the NZ Railways – who own the *Earnslaw* – belatedly decided
that the wharf wasn't sound enough to land it on. This created
an unexpected obstacle which wasn't resolved until a year later,

when we had almost decided to sell the bus. It was while a buyer was making up his mind that my son-in-law and I, after inspecting the track between Half Way Bay and Cecil Peak, decided that it might just be possible to bring the vehicle in that way. It was a bit of a risk, as if the bus failed to negotiate a couple of problem bluffs we would probably have to abandon it for good. After discussion with Lorie we determined to give it a go.

There followed a month of solid work preparing the track, working with pickaxes and shovels, levelling and widening it, and cutting out trees. We cut back scrub, bush, and lawyer vines, and tried to make the work easier by the use of the tractor and the gradall blade, but the track was so narrow and unstable that we finally had to go back to manual labour. Twice the tractor slipped over the edge when the surface gave away, and we had to winch it back up on to solid ground by an endless chain secured to a huge tree growing up the mountain above the bluffs.

When we were satisfied we had done all we could the bus was shipped to Half Way Bay Station and landed there. Lorie travelled with it, intending to bring it on up the Half Way Bay side of the river and ford it across the Lochy on to our side. But the weather was shocking, and torrential rain had made the ground a morass; before the bus had travelled a length from the wharf it was bogged to the axles. A fortnight later, when the ground was drier, I drove it on to our side of the river, taking two days to get there, and six more days to negotiate the one mile of bush and bluffs. Ten days later we had it at the homestead, a distance of eight miles all told. The successful conclusion rated a celebration, and we called the launchmaster over the radio-telephone and arranged for him to come over with some friends for the evening. We drove the bus down to the wharf to pick them up, lights all on, rather scratched and dented in places, with one or two indicators smashed or buckled, a few broken windows, and minus both rear mudguards, but otherwise beautifully roadworthy.

The following season proved the need for a second bus, and

we brought this around the same way but with much less difficulty, having blazed the trail with the first.

After we had shipped the buses to the Station, the urgency in the need for wharf repairs diminished. Earlier, when we had made plans to re-deck it in order to land the first bus, we had found that we held joint responsibility with NZ Railways for its repair and upkeep. Their responsibility was below decks, and ours above, with the exception that we had to pay for any new piles and timber requiring replacement below decks. In 1961 when we first made a move to repair the wharf, negotiations were amicable enough, and the repairs offered no problem. We were agreed on costs, with one exception: NZR required us to accept responsibility for all labour costs over a certain sum below decks. According to the terms of our contract this was specifically their responsibility and as it could involve us in the expenditure of an unknown sum which we might not be able to afford I could not see my way to accepting this clause. Thus developed a stalemate that carried over until November 1965, while the condition of the wharf steadily deteriorated.

Then NZR, after warning us of the consequences if we did not without delay agree to sign the contract, summarily closed our wharf, cutting us off from all contact with the outer world, for freight, supplies, vital farm necessities, and the operation of our business. The position was serious: not only had we to get our wool-clip out to the sales, but we had cattle to sell. Financially it was impossible to hold over either the wool-clip or the cattle for the following year, as this revenue was needed to run the Station and pay for outgoings. The tourist business which had brought over more than 13,000 people during the previous season, would be brought to a standstill as we were forbidden to land passengers on the wharf, the Department claiming that it was a "public risk".

With only one week before the closure of the wharf, we ordered a full stock of petrol, oil, and kerosene for the next 12 months, plus 10 tons of coal. On that last boat day, a greater weight than had ever before been handled was unloaded on to

the wharf in one solid pile, and the week before 90 350-lb bales
of wool had been shipped out, but the wharf showed no sign of
strain, with the exception of some of the rotten decking of which
one had to be careful.

As we hadn't quite got the last of the wool-clip away we had
to send it out by the bale on the launch *Moana*. During the
following year we experienced great inconvenience in getting
the bulky farm supplies and extra petrol and coal and supplies
in.

The preservation of our tourist business, now in its third
season, was vital too, after all the difficulties we'd had in getting
it established and becoming known; we couldn't possibly let it
remain dormant indefinitely. So during the next few weeks we
built a jetty a short distance from the main wharf, to disembark
the tourists, only to be informed that this was an illegal structure,
as we hadn't applied to the Marine Department for a permit to
build it. We hastened to fulfil this obligation, but several months
later were advised that the Marine Department did not consider
that it was up to the standard required, and it would have to be
taken down. However we were given permission to carry on
using it until the main wharf was rebuilt. By now we had found
that our new jetty was far more satisfactory than the wharf for
disembarking our passengers. It was easier for elderly or handicapped people to negotiate, so we made improvements to
comply with Marine Department requirements.

By 1966, with shearing imminent, the problem of getting our
wool-clip out assumed major proportions. We had solved the
problem of getting our cattle out for the annual sales by driving
them around the mountain, and fording the river to Half Way
Bay Station. We had co-operated with the young fellow in
charge next door in building a side to their wharf and, by using
hurdles, we were able to get the cattle away on the *Earnslaw* with
little trouble. But the freighting-out of the wool was not so
simple, and the task of trying to transport it bale by bale round
the mountain to the next-door station was far too great to consider. There was too much to go out by launch, and in any case

the lake was so abnormally low that there would be great difficulty both in getting it aboard at our wharf, and unloading it at the other end.

Fortunately, while this problem was under consideration, we managed to come to terms over the wharf. New Zealand Railways withdrew the controversial clause in the agreement, and so it was possible to accept a tender for the wharf repairs. As the work wouldn't be completed in time to ship our wool-clip out, we applied for a special dispensation to allow the steamer to call in and pick up the wool, at the same time as they were to land the equipment belonging to the contractor who was preparing to start on the wharf. After negotiations through our solicitor, and the signing of five sets of five copies of indemnities, absolving New Zealand Railways of any responsibility towards any "claims, costs, petitions, suits, actions, and demands of any kind", the *Earnslaw* was authorised to call, to leave the timber for re-decking, and to uplift the wool.

So terminated another phase of life on the "ranch".

We've had some interesting visitors. In November 1961 we were honoured with a visit of the Governor-General, Lord Cobham, and his party. Originally he was to have paid a week-end visit to fish the Lochy, but bad weather and flooding of the Oreti River delayed the viceregal party and their stay was reduced to one Sunday. I took our guests up to the Lochy in the Land-Rover. It was a dull day turning to drizzle, but fishing conditions were good, and the fish were obliging. Lady Cobham caught two beautiful rainbow weighing 6 lb, using a green-bodied fly she had made herself. His Excellency caught two, as did his sister the Hon. Mrs Grosvenor, all about the same weight. The aide, Captain Fox, a Marine commando captain, and another member of the party, Peter Wilding, fished or helped to boil the billy for a cup of tea, after an initial moment of discomfiture, when it was found that the Governor-General's rod had been inadvertently left standing against the woolshed wall when the party had come ashore from the launch.

I went bird's-nesting with the lady-in-waiting, Miss Julie Wilding, and we found six nests of black-capped tern on a stone beach. Each nest had two eggs, and the birds became very annoyed and disturbed at our approach, and made dive-bombing attacks at our heads until we moved away. Later we all went back to the homestead for cocktails and to dry out before a blazing open fire. We were bequeathed four fish from the vice-regal bag, and His Excellency declared the following day a holiday for our three boys, who were still taking Correspondence School lessons.

Another particularly enjoyable visit was that of Sir Hector and Lady MacGregor in 1964. Sir Hector, a New Zealander from Napier, and an original Battle of Britain leader, was then Commander-in-Chief of the Far East Air Force, and he was on a combined business and pleasure trip to New Zealand. We had many interests and friends in common, and Lorie and I were sorry when they had to leave.

Among other distinguished guests and fishing enthusiasts were Sir Roy and Lady Fedden, who had been out to New Zealand on fishing holidays on previous occasions, and Lord Glenconnor, Chairman of Directors of the National Mortgage and Agency, visiting New Zealand for the centennial celebrations of the company. Lord Glenconnor and his party stayed several days. We arranged for a floatplane to transport the party into Martins Bay for a day's fishing, where they caught limit bags, and the rest of their time was spent fishing the Lochy with great success.

In a different category was the visit in August 1966 of Mr Theodore C. Sorenson and his three sons, for five days' relaxation during his strenuous tour of New Zealand on a John F. Kennedy Memorial Fund Fellowship. Author of the bestseller *Kennedy*, and one-time speech-writer and legislative aide to the late President, he seemed glad to relax and catch up with his reading, while his sons, Eric, Stephen, and Philip rode, climbed, and went out on deerstalking expeditions with some of our boys.

Apart from these well-known personalities, there are occasional VIPs travelling incognito, who find the seclusion of the station and even the non-existence of our telephone "service", a definite asset. Then too there are many other charming and interesting guests, fellow New Zealanders, or hailing from all parts of the world. There was the American from Arkansas who spent three days hunting a stag, and when he found the perfect animal in his gunsights thought it was so magnificent that he laid aside his rifle and shot it with his camera instead.

When we first came to the Station the difficulties of shipping in coal twice a year, diesel oil for the lighting plant, and kerosene for heating, and the overall cost of these fuels prompted us to consider putting in our own hydro-electric plant. There was a promising-looking creek some 400 yards away from the homestead with a very high head, and this seemed the best site for our purpose. No technical difficulties were envisaged, but it would be costly, so we had to defer the idea.

However by 1964 we were so fed up with the lack of enough power for most of our needs, the constant repairs to the diesel lighting plant, the amount of work and freight and expense in procuring the means to provide only heat and light, that when an electrical contractor wrote offering to install a system we gave it consideration, and after preliminary surveys and discussions he went ahead with the job. He put in a 1,200-ft pipeline 4 in. in diameter to give a 630 ft vertical fall. The plant was for 20 kW, with a 1,500-rev. alternator. The Pelton wheel and nozzle were cast in Dunedin, and the only imported part we needed was the alternator. By November 1965 we at last had our own hydro-electric power, enough to run all the lights and electrical equipment we required.

It was a great day when the job was completed. The homestead was lit up like a Christmas tree. It was even possible to extend the power the extra one and a quarter miles to the woolshed, and so we were able to scrap the petrol-driven plant there that was always unreliable and a perfect nuisance to maintain and keep operational during shearing.

It was while the contractor was working on the hydro that he experienced the frustrations of our telephone system, and on completion of the job he offered to put a telephone cable across the lake to Queenstown. He had been employed for years by the State Power Board, and so was competent to do the job. We decided to go ahead with it, prompted by the fact that for almost a year now we had been unable to reach the Post Office at Kingston to which our line was linked.

The telephone system was another problem we had come to live with since our arrival in 1960. For some 10 years the three stations on the West side of the lake had been trying to obtain better facilities. The Post Office found it was possible to obtain good communications either by cable under the lake or by a country-set installation, but the trouble was the annual rental. By the time we came into the picture the survey had been proved practicable, but the rental was assessed at $1,200 per year. This meant $400 for each of the three stations, and we all considered this an exorbitant price for a service that costs most New Zealanders only $25.

After consideration the Post Office were persuaded to lower the rental to $60 per telephone, but each station had to install three telephones to comply with the party-line requirements, although we needed only one. This meant a rental of $180 annually, and we still considered it far too high.

In the meantime it became impossible to make any outside contact over our landline. We installed a radio-telephone, but this was satisfactory only when someone was available to take our calls. Any emergencies usually happened at night when nobody was "listening-out". At this time there were 40 permanent residents between the four stations on our side of the lake, 20 of them children, including several young babies.

Our files were bulging with letters between the Post Office, the Minister, and our local Member, but no solution was reached.

Mr Hide, the contractor, foreseeing long negotiations with the Post Office authorities, took full responsibility for the installation of the cable. He applied for licences and tried to comply with all official requirements. So on 6 September 1966 he undertook the installation at his own expense, we being committed to paying for the cable as soon as it was connected formally to the Queenstown Exchange. He chartered the launch *Muritai II* to lay the cable from Refuge Point on our property, across the lake to the far side of Queenstown Bay. The distance was about three miles, and the cable was laid at a depth of 1,200 ft. A start was made at 3.30 p.m., and it took an hour to feed out the 6,000 yards of cable over the stern of the launch. A connection was made to a telephone that Mr Hide had installed at the Queenstown end, and the first call was made.

It was loud and clear, better than any telephone call we had been able to make in all the six years we'd been at the Station, but the connections were classed as "temporary" until we received final permission from the Post Office to connect us direct to the local exchange.

However it seems that every conceivable obstacle always presents itself to prevent us achieving the most fundamental requirements and so, at the time of writing, exactly six months after the cable-laying, we are still without outside communication. The launchmaster rings us every day from the wharf over the temporary connection, but cannot ring out farther afield. The private telephone connection we have with the bureau at Kingston maintains an unbroken silence, and we note in the newspaper that the Post Office has just laid a fine new cable from Queenstown to a new housing subdivision at Kelvin Heights on the Frankton Arm for an estimated 200 subscribers, who at the moment are non-existent, the subdivisions being yet little more than surveyed line and bulldozed plots. This little proposed community has a good road access to shopping, hospital and medical facilities also, so they (when they materialise) will be luckier than we are.*

* Since the manuscript of this book was completed the telephone situation has changed. The line was finally connected to the Queenstown exchange in mid-October 1967, after much correspondence between the contractor, the Post and Telegraph Department, local MPs, and ourselves. We now have a 24-hour service, and very good speech reception.

Someone who read this book in manuscript form observed: "It all sounds as though you have a pretty tough time at Cecil Peak."

Of course we've had our tough times and perhaps I've stressed them a bit too much, but life would be pretty dull if it were all plain sailing, and that goes for everyone everywhere. Challenge is a must.

In fact, Cecil Peak has been and is our happy haven and our Shangri-la, and it's a real pleasure to share it with our visitors.

Epilogue: A Tribute

THE GREATEST ASSET AND reward any man can have in life is an understanding wife and a happy family. Well, through all the idiosyncrasies and adversities of my post-war life, I have been blessed with just that asset and reward.

My wife and I have always been one in our promotions of what most people would call way-out ideas; once I've come up with some idea I always know it will receive the full backing of Lorie's positive thinking. Nothing will daunt us, no matter how crazy the project might seem at first, and as a matter of fact, if we are ever to do all that we envisage in land and tourist development at Cecil Peak we'll not only need a hell of a lot of capital but a couple of hundred years of time into the bargain.

For a city girl Lorie has been wonderful in the way she's rapidly adapted herself to any environment. Perhaps her years as a nurse in Auckland and the years driving ambulances and big articulated trucks in the Air Force taught her the art of being adaptable. No matter what she attempts, she gives it her full and concentrated attention, and the project will surge ahead in the most positive manner.

She's been on hand as business manager of the aviation firm; using a pick and shovel on the arduous trek round the lake with the buses; interior decorating, painting, cooking, sewing, gardening, bus driving, teaching the children, helping with this book – and above all she has been and is mother, wife, and partner extraordinary.

It seems to me that the Air Force motto which lived with me during my Service years has carried over into my civilian life. When I think of all that Lorie has done – *Per Ardua ad Astra*. . . .